ROBERT WHYTE'S
1847 FAMINE SHIP DIARY

ROBERT WHYTE'S
1847 FAMINE SHIP DIARY

The Journey of an Irish Coffin Ship

Edited by

JAMES J. MANGAN

MERCIER PRESS

MERCIER PRESS

© Patrick Conroy, 1994

A CIP is available for this book from the British Library.

ISBN 1 85635 091 6

13 12 11 10 9 8

Printed in Ireland by Colour Books Ltd.

CONTENTS

PREFACE

W hyte's diary is a sort of sequel to *The Voyage of the Naparima*. It is a confirmation as well as an extension of the message that Gerald Keegan wished to extend to the world. It has the same universality of appeal for all people deprived of their basic rights as well as for those who have not known deprivation.

It has sufficient originality to merit separate attention from Keegan's diary. And it has sufficient similarity to establish the authenticity of that diary.

With all the discussion going on nowadays about the ultimate dedication of Grosse Île it should furnish enlightenment on the real meaning of this Island Graveyard.

The Appendix section brings us up to date on some of the world opinion on the thinking related to this world famous burial site of thousands of Irish immigrants.

ANN HARRISON

INTRODUCTION

Early on the morning of 20 May 1847, the Bark *Ajax* weighed anchor in Dublin harbour with over one hundred passengers on board facing a six-week crossing of the North Atlantic to what they hoped would be a land of promise somewhere in Canada. The *Ajax* was a particularly small vessel carrying a load of immigrants that would ordinarily be between five and six hundred people, far more than the rated capacity of the boat. Vessels constituting what has aptly been called the coffin fleet transported over 100,000 immigrants in panic flight from famine, fever and conditions involving deprivation of all human rights. Greedy captains and shipping agents were responsible for the crowding which resulted in much suffering and enormous loss of life on the ocean.

Within a year after landing in Canada one of the passengers of the *Ajax* published a diary that gives remarkable details about the voyage from Dublin to Grosse Île, the Canadian quarantine station. The passenger signed his name as Robert Whyte.

This diary is important for two reasons. First of all, like Gerald Keegan's diary described in *The Voyage of the Naparima* (Mangan, 1982) it tells us at first-hand what the Irish emigrant passengers endured. And secondly, in spite of the differences in the two diaries, Whyte's confirms Keegan's in the similarities of experiences met by the passengers in the coffin ships. This confirmation is important in view of the attacks that have recently been made on the authenticity of Keegan's diary, particularly in Ireland. It has, among other things, been classified as a work of fiction. There are obviously other reasons why one might reject this diary. The religious nature of the journal could be among these.

Unfortunately at present there is an attempt being made to turn Grosse Île into a national park rather than a memorial site for the tens of thousands of Irish people who lie buried there. The people behind this movement want the former quarantine station to be an historic theme park commemorating Canada as a land of welcome and hope. Those who find this unacceptable – and they are many – are concerned about the thousands who ended their lives there. Furthermore, Grosse Île is recognised by some as the most important and evocative Great Famine site on earth. There was neither welcome nor hope for the thousands who lie buried in Canada's island graveyard.

An article in the Montreal *Gazette* of 21 May 1992 expressed this concern. This article – together with an address to a Montreal panel by one of Toronto's main supporters of Grosse Île, Norita Fleming – is included at the end of the diary in the Appendix section.

The author of the diary did not identify himself in any formal kind of way, though Jordan's book, *The Grosse Île Tragedy*, claims that the observations in the diary came 'from one who was actually an eyewitness of the tragic scenes described and who, though anonymous, was a Protestant gentleman of education and position as well as a man of humane feeling and impartial observation.' On board ship he was a VIP, respected by the captain and the crew. He was apparently a professional writer intending to publish his diary. His reference to the psalms and to other inspirational writings suggests that he might even have been a cleric, though he never seems to have presided at a religious service on board. The captain, though by nature gruff, was extraordinarily deferential towards him and insisted on their eating together the meals prepared by the mistress, as she was usually called, who always travelled with him.

This diary of Whyte's is an undisputed eyewitness report submitted by a professional writer. Some of us are already wondering what the enemies of Gerald Keegan's diary will do about this book. Both diaries are plainly first-hand accounts of tragic occurrences – if we accept the part in Keegan's that was taken from the historical documents listed in the references, which are not taken from the diary.

The few changes we made are not significant. In the period in which the diary was written, it was customary to load one's text with semicolons and dashes. So we took the liberty of removing over a hundred of these distractions. We removed also a section of the text which was purely statistical and which had been referred to in other parts of the diary. In general you are being given Whyte's diary as it was published in 1848.

The name of the ship on which he travelled presented a problem. All of the ships and their sailing dates were checked. The Bark *Ajax* appears to be the most likely as it sailed on 30 May in the morning.

Shortly after Whyte landed in Canada he apparently crossed the border into the US. This was a common practice among the Irish emigrants in their anxiety to escape from the shadow of the Union Jack, seeking what they considered a refuge from British domination.

The diary appeared in print in 1848. It is signed in the author's own handwriting. Whether or not he used a pseudonym we cannot tell but it is likely that he signed his own name. In any case, this eye-witness account of an eventful voyage on an emigrant vessel is a literary gem submitted by a professional writer. It features vivid descriptions of the spectacular scenery along the St Lawrence River and striking delineations of the passengers, including the captain and his wife, the crew and the suffering travellers.

The title Whyte chose for his diary was *The Ocean Plague: The Diary of a Cabin Passenger*. In order to make the title more meaningful it was changed in this book to *Robert Whyte's 1847 Famine Ship Diary: The Journey of an Irish Coffin Ship*.

You are now invited to travel the North Atlantic on the *Ajax* and learn first hand the ordeals suffered by those 1847

11

travellers. And don't forget the Appendix sections which contain comments from the modern press on the meaning of Grosse Île and to whom it should be dedicated.

J.M.

CHAPTER I

Each moment plays
His little weapon in the narrower sphere
Of sweet domestic comfort, and cuts down
The fairest bloom of sublunary bliss.
Bliss – sublunary bliss – proud words and rain,
Implicit treason to divine decree,
A bold invasion of the rights of heaven,
I clasp'd the phantoms, and I found them air.
O, had I weighed it ere my fond embrace,
What darts of agony had miss'd my soul.

Young

30 May 1847

M any and deep are the wounds that the sensitive heart inflicts upon its possessor, as he journeys through life's pilgrimage but on few occasions are they so acutely felt as when one is about to part from those who formed a portion of his existence; deeper still pierces the pang as the idea presents itself that the separation may be for ever, but when one feels a father's nervous grasp, a dear sister's tender, sobbing embrace and the eye wanders around the apartment, drinking in each familiar object, until it rests upon the vacant chair which she who nursed his helpless infancy was wont to occupy, then the agony he wishes to conceal becomes insupportable. But as the skilful surgeon tears off the bandage which the hand of affection gently withdraws from the wound, thereby unconsciously inflicting greater pain, so it is better not to linger upon the affecting scene but rush suddenly away.

It was a charming morning on which I left dear old Ireland. The balmy new-born day in all the freshness of early summer was gladdened by the beams of the sun which rose above the towers of the city, sunk in undisturbed repose. It was a morning calculated to inspire the drooping soul with hope auguring future happiness.

Too soon I arrived at the quay and left my last footprint on my native land. The boat pushed off and in a few minutes I was on board the brig that was to waft me across the wide Atlantic.

There was not a soul on deck but presently the grizzled head of the captain was protruded from the cabin and from the uninviting aspect of his face I feared that he would prove an unsocial companion for a long voyage. He received me as kindly as his stubborn nature would allow and I was forced to admire the manly dignity of the rude tar when, from the bent attitude he was obliged to assume while ascending the companion ladder, he stood upright on the deck. The sailors now issued from the forecastle and the mate came up and introduced himself to me.

The captain having given the word to weigh anchor, a bustle immediately arose throughout the vessel; the seamen promptly proceeded to their work with apparent pleasure although (being the Sabbath) they did not accompany the action with the usual chant. The chain having become entangled in the cables of some fishing boats, it was a considerable while before the anchor was hoisted. At length the top-sails were unreefed and our bark glided through the beauteous bay.

In a short time we rounded the promontory of Howth having taken the north channel as the wind was southerly.

The captain then led me down to the cabin for breakfast and introduced me to his wife who he informed me always accompanied him to sea and whom I shall for the future designate as the mistress, as by that term she was known to both crew and passengers. Feeling an inclination towards squeamishness and being much more sick at heart, I retired to my stateroom and lying down upon the berth, fell into a dreamy slumber, in which I remained until aroused when I found it was late in the afternoon and tea was ready. I felt somewhat revived by the grateful beverage and accompanied the captain on deck. We were off Carlinford and the mountains of Mourne. The passengers were cooking their evening meal at their fires upon the fore-deck and the sailors discussing their coffee in the forecastle. I endeavoured to enter into conversation with the captain but he was provokingly taciturn; however, we were soon joined by the mistress, who was not unwilling to make up for her husband's deficiency. The sun set and twilight subsided into darkness. A cold night breeze also told that it was time to go below.

Monday, 31 May

I rose early and inhaled the fresh morning air. We made good progress during the night and the bold cliffs of the coast of Antrim were visible on one hand, the Scotch shore on the other. At 8 a.m. the bell rang for breakfast and I took my seat opposite the captain. The mistress sat in an armchair and the mate on a stool next to me, completing the cabin circle. We were attended by Simon the cabin-boy whom at first sight I took to be a 'darky'.

His face was coated with smoke and soot, streaked by the perspiration that trickled from his brow which was surmounted by a thicket of short, wiry black hair standing on end, his lustreless brown eyes I cannot better describe than by borrowing a Yankee illustration: they were 'like two glass balls lighted by weak rush lights'; his lips were thick, straight and colourless; his complexion (when unveiled) was a grimy yellow and the expression of his wide flat face, idiotic. He wore a red flannel shirt and loose blue pilot trousers but neither shoes nor stockings. His movements were slow, except at meals, when he seemed to regain his suspended animation and it was a goodly sight to see him gulping coffee, bolting dodges of fat pork and crunching hard biscuit as ravenously as a hungry bear.

No two specimens of human nature could possibly present more striking contrasts than Simon and his fellow apprentice, Jack. The latter was about 15 years of age, remarkably small and active. Squirrel never climbed a tree more nimbly than Jack could go aloft, and in the accomplishment of chewing and smoking he might compete with the oldest man aboard. His fair skin was set off by rosy cheeks and his sparkling blue eyes beamed with devilment. He was a favourite of everyone – except the mistress, with whom his pranks did not pass – being therefore exempt from the menial offices of cabin boy which devolved upon Simon. His principal amusement consisted in persecuting that genius.

The mate was a very little man not more than five feet high but in excellent condition, as seamen generally are. He was lame in one leg which deformity he took great pains to hide, causing a constrained limp that was extremely ludicrous. He was well-looking and sported a capacious pair of black whiskers, the outline of which he frequently altered. He had been a 'captain' but unfortunately, loving the bottle, he lost his 'cast'. There existed little confidence between him and the captain and, both being of a warm temperament, there were occasional symptoms of collision but they were prevented from ending in open rapture by the timely interference of the mistress, on whom the captain would let loose his wrath, which though expressed in no gentle terms she bore with exemplary patience.

The mistress was small, ruddy and sun-burnt, having seen some sixty winters, forty of which she had spent at sea, generally in the home trade but varied occasionally by voyage to Russia or to America. She was in the habit of keeping a private log, in which she noted the incidents of her travels. I was allowed to look into this interesting production, which amused me no less by the originality of the orthography, than its elegance of diction. Being a native of Cumberland her pronunciation was not particularly euphonious. She also, when addressing her husband, the mate and all familiar acquaintances, used the terms 'thee' and 'thou' invariably reversing their grammatical order.

After breakfast, the mate invited me to see the depot of provisions. I accordingly followed him, descending by a ladder into an apartment partitioned off from the hold, and dividing it from the cabin.

By the light from the lantern I perceived a number of sacks, which were filled with oatmeal and biscuit. The mate having proceeded to prepare the passengers' rations for distribution, I sat down upon one of the sacks, from beneath which suddenly issued a groan. I jumped up, quite at a loss to account for the strange sound and looked at the mate in order to discover what he thought of it. He seemed somewhat surprised but in a moment removed two or three sacks and lo! there was a man crouched up in a corner. As he had not seen him before, the mate at once concluded that he was a 'stowaway', so giving him a shake to make him stand upright, he ordered him to mount the ladder, bestowing a kick upon the poor wretch to accelerate his tardy ascent.

The captain was summoned from below and a council immediately held for the trial of the prisoner, who confessed that, not having enough of money to pay for his passage, he bribed the watchman employed to prevent the possibility of such an occurrence. He had been concealed for three days but at night made his way into the hold, through a breach in the partition; His presence was therefore known to some of the passengers. He had no clothes but the rags he wore nor had he any provisions. To decide what was to be done with him was now the consideration, but the captain hastily terminated the deliberation by swearing that he should be thrown overboard. The wretched creature was quite discomfited by the captain's wrath and earnestly begged for forgiveness. It was eventually settled that he should be landed upon the first island at which we should touch, with which

17

decision he appeared to be quite satisfied. He said that he was willing to work for his support but the captain swore determinedly that he should not taste one pound of the ship's provision. He was therefore left to the tender mercies of his fellow passengers.

In consequence of this discovery, there was a general muster in the afternoon, affording me an opportunity of seeing all the emigrants – and a more motley crowd I never beheld; of all ages, from the infant to the feeble grandsire and withered crone.

While they were on deck, the hold was searched, but without any further discovery, no one having been found below but a boy who was unable to leave his berth from debility. Many of them appeared to me to be quite unfit to undergo the hardship of a long voyage, but they were inspected and passed by a doctor, although the captain protested against taking some of them. One old man was so infirm that he seemed to me to be in the last stage of consumption.

The next matter to be accomplished was to regulate the allowance of provisions to which each family was entitled, one pound of meal or of bread being allowed for each adult, half a pound for each individual under fourteen years of age, and one-third of a pound for each child under seven years. Thus, although there were 110 souls, great and small, they counted as 84 adults. That was, therefore, the number of pounds to be issued daily. On coming on board, provisions for a week were distributed but as they wasted them most improvidently, they had to be served again today. The mate consequently determined to give out the day's rations every morning.

Wednesday, 2 June

We made but little progress during the night and were still in the channel, within sight of the Mull of Kintyre and the northern shore of Ireland.

Having but a few books with me, I seized upon a greasy old volume of sundry magazines, which I found in the cabin. I also commenced the study of a book of navigation. These, varied with the Book of books, Shakespeare and *Maunder's Treasuries*, kept me free from ennui. When tired of reading, I had ample scope for observation.

The mistress spent the forenoon fishing, and the afternoon in curing the mackerel and gurnet she caught. We had some at tea when I met with a deprivation I had not anticipated – there was no milk! and I did not at all relish my tea without it. One cup was quite enough for me, but I soon became habituated to it. Having rounded the long promontory of Donegal, the outline of the shore became indistinct and, making our calculations not to see land again for some time, the mate took his 'departure' from Malin Head.

CHAPTER II

Roll on, thou dark and deep blue blue ocean, roll!

Byron

Thursday, 3 June

When I came on deck this morning I found that we were sailing upon the bosom of the broad Atlantic, no object being visible to relieve the vast expanse of water and sky, except the glorious sun and as I turned my eyes from the survey of the distant horizon and fixed them upon the little bark that wafted us, a sensation akin to that of the 'Ancient Mariner' possessed my mind.

> Alone, alone, all, all alone,
> Alone on a wide, wide sea.

As the boy who was unable to attend the muster still continued ill, and was reported to be feverish, the mistress and I reviewed the medicine chest. We found it to contain a jar of castor oil, Epsom salts, laudanum, hartshorn, etc; also a book of directions, which were by no means explicit, and they so perplexed the mistress, even with the aid of her spectacles, that as she was nothing the wiser of the study she resolved to trust to her own experience in the concoction of a dose. The mate took his first observation at noon and as he stood peering through the eye-hole of the quadrant, he reminded me forcibly of poor old Uncle Sol's little midshipman.

The passengers' fireplaces, upon either side of the fore-deck furnished endless scenes, sometimes of noisy merriment, at others of quarrels. The fire was contained in a large wooden case lined with bricks and shaped something like an old-fashioned settee – the coals being confined by two or three iron bars in front. From morning till evening they were surrounded by groups of men, women and children; some making stirabout in all kinds of vessels, and others baking cakes upon extemporary griddles. These cakes were generally about two inches thick, and when baked were encased in a burnt crust coated with smoke, being actually raw in the centre. Such was the unvaried food of the greater number of these poor creatures. A few of them, who seemed to be better off, had herrings or bacon. The meal with which they were provided was of very bad quality – this they had five days and biscuit, which was good, two days in the week.

Friday, 4 June

The sailors and apprentices were (as the mate expressed it in his log) variously employed mending sails, tarring ropes, spinning yarns, etc. Sailors sit and sew very differently from tailors; instead of doubling up their legs under them they stretch them out straight before them as they sit upon the deck. Their thimble is also peculiar, not being worn on the top of the finger, but upon the ball of the thumb, to which it is fastened by a leather strap, buckled round the wrist. I was surprised at the expedition and neatness with which they sewed with their coarse needles and long threads.

Jack created some diversion by daubing a gossoon's face with tar, and shaving him with a rusty knife. It was exhilarating to hear the children's merry laughter – poor little things, they seemed quite reconciled with their situation! I learned that many of these emigrants had never seen the sea nor a ship until they were on board. They were chiefly from the County Meath, and sent out at the expense of their landlord without any knowledge of the country to which they were going, or means of livelihood except the labour of the father of each family. All they knew concerning Canada was that they were to land in Quebec and to go up the country; moreover, they had a settled conviction that the voyage was to last exactly three weeks. In addition to these, there were a few who were going to try their fortunes on their own account. One of the latter was a Connaught 'boy', who having lived upon the coast and spent his time partly in fishing, made himself useful about the brig and thereby ingratiated himself into favour with the captain and won the consequent jealousy of his fellow passengers, who, thinking him rather soft, took pleasure in teasing him. Two young men from Kilkenny and one from the County Clare completed the list. The former used to astonish the Meath-men with the triple wonders of their native city.

Saturday, 5 June

As the passengers had a great inclination to infringe upon the after-deck, the captain drew a line, the penalty for crossing which was the stoppage of a day's water.

I observed the sea to be crowded with myriads of slimy looking objects, which the sailors called 'slobbs'. They varied in size, form, and colour, some of them resembling a lemon cut in half. How beautiful also was the luminous appearance of the water at night, which I delighted to watch, as we glided through the liquid fire.

Nor was it less pleasing to observe the 'Portuguese men of war', with their tiny sails set to the breeze, and surmounting the crests of the rolling billows. I had a rummage through the charts and enjoyed a practical lecture upon them, with illustrative lectures by the mistress, enlivened by way of episode with occasional contradictions by the captain who with rule and compass traced our progress daily upon the great chart of the North Atlantic ocean. We had two ships in company with us all the day; they were too distant to distinguish their names. One of the passengers having thrown the Connaughtman's hat overboard, the captain gave him a blue and white striped night-cap, with which on his head he strutted about, much to the amusement of the youngsters, one of whom attached a rope to the tail of his coat; this he dragged after him for some time, until Jack changed the scene by cutting the tail off. When Paddy discovered his loss, he was outraged and made a grievous complaint to the mate who doctored the coat by abstracting the other tail, thereby transforming the garment into a jacket. When the matter came to the captain's ears he presented Paddy with an old pilot jacket, which made a great coat for him; he was, therefore, no loser by the affair.

Sunday, 6 June

The favourable breeze that carried us out of the channel having forsaken us, the little progress we made was gained by tacking, which kept the sailors constantly employed. The passengers were dressed in their best clothes and presented a better appearance then I expected. The sailors also donned their holiday toggery in the afternoon.

A group of young men, being at a loss for amusement, began to wrestle and play 'pitch and toss' but the mate soon put a stop to their diversions at which they grumbled, saying that they 'didn't think that Mr Mate would be so hard'.

Very few of them could read; neither did they seem to have any regard for the sanctity of the Sabbath. In the evening they had prayers in the hold and were divided into two parties – those who spoke Irish, and those who did not; each section having a leader who gabbled in his respective language a number of 'Paters and Aves', as quickly as the devotees could count their beads.

After these religious exercises they came upon deck and spent the remainder of the day jesting, laughing and singing.

We had a clear and beautiful sunset from which the captain prognosticated an easterly wind.

CHAPTER III

Monday, 7 June

The passengers elected four men to govern their commonwealth, the principal of whom had the title of 'head committee'. The other three being inactive, the sole authority was wielded by him much to the terror of the little boys who were often uproarious and to keep whom in order he frequently administered the 'cat'.

The other duties of this functionary consisted in seeing that the hold was kept clean, in preventing smoking below, settling differences, etc. He was also the medium of communication with the 'other house' – he and Paddy alone being permitted to go aft.

Tuesday, 8 June

We steered a southward course but gained very little longitude.

The two ships were again in sight, one was the *Tamerlane* of Aberystwyth, the other the *Virginius* of Liverpool; both fine vessels with passengers.

The head committee reported that two women were ill. They were therefore dosed according to the best skills of the mistress, who was desirous of going into the hold to see them, but the captain peremptorily desired her upon no account to do so and kept a sharp lookout that she might not visit them unknown to him.

The boy, whom nothing ailed but seasickness and

fatigue, had recovered. I saw him upon deck – miserable looking little animal, with a huge misshapen head, sallow, lantern-jaws and glassy eyes – apparently about twelve years of age; but his father said that he was twenty. I could scarcely credit him but was assured of the fact by his neighbours who said that he always had the same emaciated appearance, although he never before complained of illness. He went by the name of 'the little shoemaker'.

Wednesday, 9 June

As we were seated at dinner in the cabin discussing a savoury dish of lobscouse made by the mistress, we were alarmed by the shouting of men and screaming of women.

We hurried on deck, thinking that someone was overboard and judge of our terror when we saw the fore part of the brig in a blaze. All hands having assisted, a plentiful supply of water in a short time subdued the fire which extended no further than the caboose; it arose from the negligence of Simon who fell asleep leaving a lighted candle stuck against the boards. This was the only brilliant act of which he was guilty during the voyage and as a reward for which the mate bestowed upon him a rope's end.

Thursday, 10 June

The only incidents of the day were breakfast, dinner and supper – and the meridional observation and the temporary stir consequent on the captain coming upon deck after a snooze, and shouting, ''bout ship'. Some more cases of illness were reported and the mistress was kept busy mixing medicine and making drinks, hoping that by early attention the sickness might be prevented from spreading.

As I was pacing the deck in the afternoon I observed one of the passengers – a well-looking man with fine brown eyes – timidly approach me. After looking about him to assure himself that the captain was below, he doffed his hat and addressed me as follows: 'I beg your honour's pardon, but I hope it's no offence.' Having told him that he had given me none, he proceeded – 'Well then, Master, isn't it mighty quare intirely and how can the likes of us know the differ; but I hope your honour it's all right?'

I replied that I was not aware of anything being wrong and desired him to say what was the danger he feared which caused him to ask: 'Aragh! Why thin are we goin' back to ould Ireland?' I demanded his reason for such a supposition when, after scratching his head and casting a glance towards the cabin, looking rather perplexed, he went on. 'That little gossoon of mine, your honour – a mighty smart chap he is too and a great scholar entirely, he tould us – but faith! I dunno how to believe him though he got his larnin' at the national school and can cast up figures equal to the agent and can read the whole side of a book without stoppin'. He says, sir, that the sun, God bless it, sets in the wist ...'

Here he paused and looked earnestly at me, as if for confirmation of the fact. I therefore said that the boy's knowledge was pretty accurate.

Seeming encouraged, he continued – 'Moreover than that, he says that Ameriky, where we are goin' to, if the Almighty God spares us. (Here he crossed himself.) Glory be to his name! it's in the wist of the world too.' He again paused and looked enquiringly.

'Well,' said I, 'he is pretty right there also, America is west from Ireland.'

'Then, Master, here's what we want to come at, you see. If Ameriky is in the wist, mustn't the sun set in it? Then why is it your honour, that instead of followin' it, we're runnin' away from it as hard as we can lick?'

Such was the fact – a fresh northerly breeze compelling us to bear to the south-east. I now saw the nature of the problem he wished to have solved and explained the matter as explicitly as I possibly could but it was some time before he comprehended me. At length he seemed to become enlightened on the subject, for, giving his thigh a slap of his open palm, he exclaimed: 'Och! By the powers, I see it all now, it's as plain as a pike-start and I'm sure I'm obleeged to your honour and so is the gossoon too. Oh, that divil's clip – Jack – wait till I ketch him. If I don't murder him it's not matter. What do you think, your honour, he tould the little chap, when he axed him all about it? "Why," says he, "sure we're goin' back again for the mistress' knittin' needles that she forgot." So as he wouldn't tell him, nor none of the sailors, I made bould to ax your honour as the little chap was loath to make so free.'

On the conclusion of the dialogue, Jack, who was over our heads in the shrouds, burst into a hearty fit of laughter, in which I could not but participate when I noticed the comicality of the arch sailor-boy's appearance and the simplicity of my interlocutor, who, hearing the captain's heavy step coming up the ladder, hastily retired, vowing vengeance upon Jack.

Saturday, 12 June

I amused myself taking a sketch of the cabin 'interior'. It was about ten feet square and so low that the only part of it in which the captain could stand upright was under the skylight. At either side was a berth, both of which were filled with the mistress' boxes, the captain's old clothes, old sails and sundry other articles, which were there stowed away and concealed from view by chintz curtains trimmed with white cotton fringe.

The ceiling was garnished with numerous charts rolled

27

up and confined by tapes running from beam to beam, from one of which – carefully covered by a cotton handkerchief – was suspended the captain's new hat.

A small recess above the table contained a couple of wine glasses, one of them minus the shank; also an antique decanter resting upon an old quarto prayer book and guarded by a dangerous looking blunderbuss, which was supported by two brass hooks, from one of which hung a small bag containing the captain's spectacles, rule, pencil and compass. At each side of this recess was a locker, one of them containing a crock of butter and another of effects besides tobacco and soap; the other held a fine Cheshire cheese, a little keg of sprats and other articles too numerous to mention.

An unhappy canary, perched within a rusty cage, formed a pendant from the centre of the skylight, but a much more pleasing picture decorated one of the panels – a still-life admirably delineating an enormous flitch of bacon which daily grew less.

A small door led into the captain's state-room the ceiling of which was tastefully ornamented by several bunches of dipped candles, while the narrow shelves groaned under the weight of jars of sugar, preserves, bottled porter, spices and the other usual necessaries for a long voyage. I was disturbed in the progress of my portraiture by the mistress who came down to warm a drink at the stove for some of the sick folks. The two women who first became ill were said to show symptoms of bad fever and additional cases of illness were reported by the head committee. The patients begged for an increased allowance of water, which could not be granted as the supply was very scanty, two casks having leaked.

Sunday, 13 June

The reports from the hold became very alarming and the mistress was occupied all day attending the numerous calls upon her. She already regretted having come on the voyage, but her kind heart did not allow her to consult her case. When she appeared upon deck she was beset by a crowd of poor creatures, each having some request to make, often of a most inconsiderate kind and few of which it was in her power to comply with. The day was cold and cheerless and I occupied myself reading in the cabin.

Monday, 14 June

The head committee brought a can of water to show it to the captain; it was quite foul, muddy and bitter from having been in a wine cask. When allowed to settle it became clear, leaving considerable sediment in the bottom of the vessel but it retained its bad taste. The mate endeavoured to improve it by trying the effect of charcoal and of alum but some of the casks were beyond remedy and the contents, when pumped out, resembles nauseous ditch water. There were now eight cases of serious illness – six of them being fever and two dysentery. The former appeared to be of a peculiar character and very alarming, the latter disease did not seem to be so violent in degree.

Tuesday, 15 June

The reports this morning were very afflicting and I felt much that I was unable to render any assistance to my poor fellow passengers. The captain desired the mistress to give them everything out of his own stores that she considered would be of service to any of them. He felt much alarmed; nor was it to be wondered at that contagious fever – which under the most advantageous circumstances and under the watchful eyes of the most skilful physicians, baffles the highest ability – should terrify one having the charge of so many human beings likely to fall a prey to the unchecked progress of the dreadful disease; for once having shown itself in the unventilated hold of a small brig, containing one hundred and ten living creatures, how could it possibly be stayed without medicines, medical skill or even pure water to slake the patients' burning thirst?

The prospect before us was indeed an awful one and there was no hope for us but in the mercy of God.

Wednesday, 16 June

The past night was very rough and I enjoyed little rest. No additional cases of sickness were reported, but there were apparent signs of insubordination amongst the healthy men, who complained of starvation and the want of water to make drinks for their sick wives and children. A deputation came aft to acquaint the captain with their grievances but he ordered them away and would not listen to a word from them. When he went below the ringleader threatened that they would break into the provision store.

The mate did not take any notice of the threat but repeated to me, in their hearing, an anecdote of his own experience, of a captain, showing with what determination he suppressed an outbreak in his vessel. He concluded by alluding to cut-lasses and the firearms in the cabin. And in order to make a deeper impression on their minds he brought up the old blunderbuss from which be fired a shot, the report of which was equal to that of a small cannon. The deputation slunk away muttering complaints.

If they were resolute they might easily have seized upon the provisions. In fact, I was surprised how famished men could so patiently bear with their own and their starved children's sufferings, but the captain would willingly have listened to them if it were in his power to relieve their distress.

Two new cases of fever were announced and, from the representation of the mate, the poor creatures in the hold were in a shocking state. The men who suffered from dysentery were better; the mistress' prescription – flour porridge with a few drops of laudanum – having given them relief. The requests of the friends of the fever patients were most preposterous, some asking for beef, others wine. They were all desirous of laudanum being administered to them in order to procure sleep but we were afraid to dispense so dangerous a remedy except with extreme caution.

Our progress was almost imperceptible and the captain began to grow very uneasy, there being at the rate of the already miserable allowance of food, but provisions for 50 days. It also now became necessary to reduce the complement of water and to urge the necessity of using sea water in cookery.

The fireplaces were the scenes of endless contentions. The sufferings they endured appeared to embitter the wretched emigrants one against another. Their quarrels were only ended when the fires were extinguished at 7 p.m. at which time they were surrounded by squabbling groups preparing their miserable evening meal. They would not leave until Jack mounted the shrouds of the foremast and precipitated a bucket full of water on each fire – when they snatched up their pots and pans and, half blinded by the steam, descended into the hold with their half-cooked suppers. Although Jack delighted in teasing them, they never complained of his pranks, however annoying.

CHAPTER IV

I saw the seven angels which stood before God; and to
them were given seven trumpets ...
And the seven angels which had the seven trumpets
prepared themselves to sound ...
And the seventh angel sounded ...
And the sea gave up the dead which were in it; and
death and hell delivered up the dead which were in them
and they were judged every man ...

Revelations

Saturday, 19 June

A shark followed us all the day and the mate said it
was a certain forerunner of death. The cabin was like
an apothecary's shop and the mistress a perfect
slave. I endeavoured to render her every assistance in my
power. The mate also was indefatigable in his exertions to
alleviate the miserable lot of our helpless human cargo.

Not having seen the stowaway on deck for some time,
upon inquiring after him, I learned that he was amongst the
sick and was very bad but he was kindly attended by the
young man from the County Clare who devoted himself to
attending the afflicted, some of whom the members of their
own families neglected to take care of.

Sunday, 20 June

Having hinted to the captain the propriety of having
divine service read upon the Sabbath, he said that it
could not be done. Indeed the sailors seldom had a spare
moment and as to the mate, I often wondered how he got
through so much work. This day, therefore, had no mark to
distinguish it from any other. The poor emigrants were in
their usual squalid attire, neither did the crew rig themselves
out as on former Sundays.

All were dispirited and a cloud of melancholy hung over us.

The poor mistress deplored that she could not get an opportunity of reading her Bible. I pitied her from my heart knowing how much she felt the distress that surrounded us and her anxiety to lighten the affliction of the passengers.

Monday, 21 June

I was surprised at the large allowance of food served out to the sailors. They had each 1–2lbs of beef or pork daily, besides coffee and as much biscuit as they pleased, but it being a temperance vessel, they had no grog, in lieu of which they got lime-juice. However, there was a little cask of brandy in a corner of the cabin but the captain was afraid to broach it, knowing the mate's propensity. I noticed the latter often casting a wistful glance at it as he rose from dinner and he did not fail to tell me that it was the best possible preventive against the fever.

Tuesday, 22 June

One of the sailors was unable for duty and the mate feared he had the fever.

The reports from the hold were growing even more alarming and some of the patients who were mending, had relapsed. One of the women was every moment expected to breathe her last and her friends – an aunt and cousins – were inconsolable about her as they had persuaded her to leave her father and mother and come with them.

The mate said that her feet were swollen to double their natural size and covered with black putrid spots. I spent a considerable part of the day watching a shark that followed in our wake with great constancy.

At breakfast, I inquired of the mate after the young woman who was so ill yesterday, when he told me that she was dead and when I remarked that I feared her burial could cause great consternation, I learned that the sad ordeal was over, her remains having been consigned to the deep within an hour after she expired. When I went on deck I heard the moans of her poor aunt who continued to gaze upon the ocean as if she could mark the spot where the waters opened for their prey. The majority of the wretched passengers who were not themselves ill were absorbed in grief for their relatives, but some of them, it astonished me to perceive, had no feeling whatever, either for their fellow creatures' woe or in the contemplation of being themselves overtaken by the dreadful disease. There was further addition to the sick list which now amounted to twenty.

Being the festival of St John and a Catholic holiday, some young men and women got up a dance in the evening regardless of the moans and cries of those who were tortured by the fiery fever. When the mate spoke to them of the impropriety of such conduct, they desisted and retired to the bow where they sat down and spent the remainder of the evening singing. The monotonous howling they kept up was quite in unison with the scene of desolation within and the dreary expanse of ocean without.

This morning there was a further accession to the names upon the sick roll. It was awful how suddenly some were stricken. A little child who was playing with its companions, suddenly fell down and for some time was sunk in a death-like torpor from which, when she awoke, she commenced to scream violently and writhed in convulsive agony. A poor woman, who was warming a drink at the fire for her husband, also dropped down quite senseless and was borne to her berth.

I found it very difficult to acquire precise information respecting the progressive symptoms of the disease, the different parties of whom I inquired disagreeing in some particulars, but I inferred that the first symptom was generally a reeling in the head, followed by swelling pain, as if the head were going to burst. Next came excruciating pains in the bones and then swelling of the limbs commencing with the feet, in some cases ascending the body and again descending before it reached the head, stopping at the throat. The period of each stage varied in different patients, some of whom were covered with yellow, watery pimples and others with red and purple spots that turned into putrid sores.

Saturday, 26 June

Some of those who the other day appeared to bid defiance to the fever, were seized in its relentless grasp and a few who were on the recovery, relapsed. It seemed miraculous to me that such subjects could struggle with so violent a disease without any effective aid.

Sunday, 27 June

The moaning and raving of the patients kept me awake nearly all the night and I could hear the mistress stirring about until a late hour. It made my heart bleed to listen to the cries for 'Water, for God's sake some water'. Oh! it was horrifying, yet strange to say I had no fear of taking the fever, which, perhaps, under the merciful providence of the Almighty was a preventive cause. The mate, who spent much of his time among the patients, described to me some

35

revolting scenes he witnessed in the hold but they were too disgusting to be repeated. He became very much frightened and often looked quite bewildered.

Monday, 28 June

The number of patients upon the list now amounted to thirty and the effluvium of the hold was shocking.

The passengers suffered much for want of pure water and the mate tried the quality of all the casks.

Fortunately he discovered a few which were better and the circumstance was rather cheering.

Tuesday, 29 June

The wind kept us to the south but though occasionally becalmed, we were slowly gaining longitude.

I could not keep my mind fixed upon a book so I was obliged to give over reading and spent the day watching the rolling of the dolphin, the aerial darts of the flying-fish with the gambols of numbers of porpoises that danced in the waters around the prow. It being the mate's watch, I remained upon deck until midnight, listening to his yarns. Some of them were rather incredible and, upon expressing such to be my opinion, he was inclined to take offence. Being the hero of some of his stories himself, I could not doubt the veracity of them, though they were not the least marvellous. Although a well informed and intelligent man, he was very superstitious. But it is not uncommon for sailors to be so.

Wednesday, 30 June

Passing the main hatch, I got a glimpse of one of the most awful sights I ever beheld. A poor female patient was lying in one of the upper berths – dying. Her head and face were swollen to almost unnatural size, the latter being hideously deformed. I recollected remarking the clearness of her complexion when I saw her in health, shortly after we sailed. She then was a picture of good humour and contentment, now how sadly altered! Her cheeks retained their ruddy hue but the rest of her distorted countenance was of a leprous whiteness. She had been nearly three weeks ill and suffered exceedingly until the swelling set in, commencing in her feet and creeping up her body to her head. Her afflicted husband stood by her holding a 'blessed candle' in his hand and awaiting the departure of her spirit. Death put a period to her existence shortly after I saw her. And as the sun was setting, the bereaved husband muttered a prayer over her enshrouded corpse which, as he said Amen, was lowered into the ocean.

Thursday, 1 July

The wind was still unfavourable but we gained a little by constantly tacking and were approaching the banks of Newfoundland. Some new cases were announced making thirty-seven now lying. A convalescent was assisted on deck and seemed revived by the fresh air. He was a miserable object. His face, being yellow and withered, was rendered ghastly by the black streak that encircled his sunken eyes.

CHAPTER V

We were enveloped in a dense fog and had a horn sounding constantly. One of the patients, who was represented to be dying, sent for the mate and, giving him the key of his box in which there was a small sum of money, requested him to take charge of it and, upon his return to Ireland, send it to his (the sick man's) mother.

The mate promised to do so but did not consider the poor fellow as bad as he himself feared he was.

Saturday, 3 July

Any idea I ever formed of complete horror was excelled by the stern reality of the frightful picture which the past night presented. The gloom spread around by the impenetrable fog was heightened by the dismal tone of the foghorn, between each sound of which might be heard the cries and ravings of the delirious patients and occasionally the tolling of a bell, warning us of the vicinity of some fishing-boat, numbers of which were scattered over the banks.

The mate being unable to make an observation, we were obliged to depend upon his 'dead reckoning'.

Sunday, 4 July

We enjoyed a favourable breeze, and the fog having cleared off at noon, the mate made an observation, by which we were in 45° 11' N lat, 51° 10' W lon. No new cases of sickness were reported but some of the patients were said to be very bad.

We spoke to a bark and a brig, both homeward bound and differed but little in longitude. There was something exciting in listening to the friendly voice from the deep toned speaking trumpet and in beholding the board marked with the longitude. In a few moments the ensigns were lowered and each pursued its course.

The day was exceedingly cold, so much so that the captain supposed that we were in the neighbourhood of icebergs and I hoped to see one of these castellated floating masses, lifting its pinnacles on high and glittering in the rays of the sun.

Monday, 5 July

The morning was foggy and we were near running into a French fishing boat.

The captain having given orders for sounding, Jack was sent to find the reel and line, which he brought up from the depths of the lazaretto. This receptacle for all sorts of commodities was situated below the cabin and it afforded me some amusement to see the boy, by the faint light of the lantern, groping among beef casks, pork barrels, paint and tar pots, spars and rusty irons. The sails having been put aback so that the brig stood motionless upon the bosom of the water, the reel was held by a man at the stern and the line being uncoiled was drawn outside the ropes of the rigging, until it reached the bow. The lead was then attached and carried by a seaman to the point of bowsprit, where the sailor sat swinging the weight like a pendulum until, upon the order to heave, he cast it forth upon its mission. Bottom having been found at thirty-four fathoms, the line was placed upon a pulley and drawn up when there was found imbedded in the grease with which the lead was filled, fine white sand, as laid down in the chart.

The sails were again set to the breeze and we were once more gliding through the water, the momentary commotion soon settling down into the usual insanity.

Tuesday, 6 July

During the past night there was a heavy fall of rain which left the atmosphere clear and cool.

Two men (brothers) died of dysentery and I was awakened by the noise made by the mate, who was searching for an old sail to cover the remains with. In about an hour after, they were consigned to the deep, a remaining brother being the solitary mourner. He continued long to gaze upon the ocean, while a tear that dropped from his moistened eye told the grief he did not otherwise express. I learned in the afternoon that he was suffering from the same complaint that carried off his brothers.

Wednesday, 7 July

The phosphorescent appearance of the ocean at night was very beautiful. We seemed to be gliding through a sea of liquid fire. We passed a great number of fishing boats, chiefly French, from the isles St Pierre and Miquelon.

They were anchored at regular intervals for the purpose of catching cod-fish, which, allured by the vast numbers of worms found upon the bottom, abound upon the banks.

The vessels generally are large sloops and have a platform all round with an awning over the deck. When a fish is taken, it is immediately split and cleaned, then it is thrown into the hold and, when the latter is full, the fishermen return home and land their cargo to be dried and saved.

Owing to these processes being sometimes too long deferred, the bank fish, though larger, is considered inferior to that taken along the coast of Newfoundland.

Great variety of opinion exists respecting the nature and origin of these submarine banks but none of them appears to me so natural as this. The stream which issues from the Gulf of Mexico, commonly called the 'Florida gulf stream', being checked in its progress by the southern coast of Newfoundland, deposits the vast amount of matter held in suspension. This, by accumulation, formed the banks which are still increasing in extent. The temperature of the water upon the banks is higher than that of the Gulf of St Lawrence and of the ocean and its evaporation causes the fog that almost perpetually prevails.

The afternoon was clear with a gentle breeze which formed a ripple on the surface of the water and gave a beautiful appearance to the reflection of the declining sun, looking like jets of gas bursting from the deep.

Thursday, 8 July

A nother of the crew was taken ill, thereby reducing our hands when they were most required. The captain had a great dread of the coast of Newfoundland which, being broken into deep bays divided from each other by rocky capes, is rendered exceedingly perilous, more especially, as the powerful currents set towards this inhospitable shore.

We kept a lookout for some vessel coming from the gulf, in order to learn the bearings of land but did not perceive one during the day.

Friday, 9 July

A few convalescents appeared upon deck. The appearance of the poor creatures was miserable in the extreme. We now had fifty sick, being nearly one half the whole number of passengers. Some entire families, being prostrated, were dependent on the charity of their neighbours, many of whom were very kind, but others seemed to be possessed of no feeling. Among the former, the head committee was conspicuous.

The brother of the two men who died on the sixth instant

followed them today. He was seized with dismay from the time of their death, which no doubt hurried on the malady to its fatal termination. The old sails being all used up, his remains were placed in two meal-sacks and a weight being fastened at foot, the body was placed upon one of the hatch battens from which, when raised over the bulwark, it fell into the deep and was no more seen. He left two little orphans, one of whom – a boy, seven years of age – I noticed in the evening wearing his deceased father's coat. Poor little fellow! He seemed quite unconscious of his loss and proud of the accession to his scanty covering. The remainder of the man's clothes were sold by auction by a friend of his who promised to take care of the children. There was great competition and the 'Cant', as they called it, occasioned jibing and jesting, which it was painful to listen to surrounded as were the actors (some of whom had just risen from a bed of sickness), by famine, pestilence and death.

CHAPTER VI

The floods are risen. O Lord, the floods have lifted up
their voice: the floods lift up their waves. The waves
of the sea are mighty and rage horribly: but yet the
Lord who dwelleth on high is mightier.

David

Saturday, 10 July

We spoke to a wherry which was conveying cattle from Nova Scotia to Newfoundland and learned from the steersman the bearings of St Paul's Island. We shortly afterwards passed a large fleet coming from the gulf and in the afternoon descried Cape North.

The passengers expressed great delight at seeing land and were under the impression that they were near their destination, little knowing the extent of the gulf they had to pass and the great river to ascend. Early in the evening we saw Isle St Paul and indistinctly the point of Cape Ray, between which and Cape North is the passage into the Gulf of St Lawrence. St Paul's Island lies about ten miles to the north of the latter cape, in latitude 47° 14′ North and longitude 60° 11′ 17′ West. It is a huge rock, dividing at top into three conical peaks. Rising boldly from the sea there is a great depth of water all round it and vessels may pass at either side of it. It has been the site of numerous shipwrecks; many vessels carried out of their reckoning by the currents, having been dashed against it when concealed by fog and instantly shattered to atoms.

Human bones and other memorials of these disasters are strewn around its base. We passed the light of this dangerous island at 10 p.m. entering into the 'goodly great gulf full of islands, passages and entrances towards what wind soever you please to bend'.

This gulf was first explored by John Cabot in 1497, who

43

called the coast of Labrador Primarista. The Portuguese afterwards changed the name of that desert region to Terra Coterealis and the gulf they designated as that of the 'Two Brothers' in memory of Gaspar and Michael Cotereal, the first named of whom not having returned from the second expedition he commanded, the latter went in search of him, but neither of them was afterwards heard of.

Jaques Cartier, having entered it upon the festival of St Lawrence, gave to the gulf and the river flowing into it the name they still retain.

Sunday, 11 July

We had a fair wind and were going full sail at 7 knots an hour. At noon we passed the Bird Islands which are low ledges of rocks and swarm with gannets, numbers of which were flying about. They were as large as geese and pure white with the exception of the tips of the wings which were jet black. Some of Mother Carey's chickens were following in our wake and it was highly amusing to watch the contentions of the little creatures for bits of fat thrown to them.

We had a distant view of the Magdalen Islands which, although lying nearer to Nova Scotia, are considered as belonging to Canada and form a portion of the circuit within the district of Gaspé, court being held at Amherst harbour annually from 1 to 10 July. The largest of the group are Bryon, Deadman's, Amherst, Entry and Wolf islands which are inhabited by a hardy race of fishermen. The huge walrus may at times be seen upon their shores.

Monday, 12 July

In the morning we were becalmed, the water being smooth as glass and of a beautifully clear, green hue.

A breeze sprung up at 12 o'clock and, the captain having

provided himself and me with lines, we spent the afternoon fishing for mackerel, which were so plentiful that I caught seventy in about two hours, when I had to give over, my hands being cut by the line. The captain continued and had a barrel full by evening. They were the finest mackerel I ever saw and we had some at tea which we all enjoyed as a delicious treat after six weeks of salt beef and biscuit diet. Many of the passengers, having noticed our success, followed our example and lines were out from every quarter; all the twine, thread, etc. that could be made out being put into requisition, with padlocks and bolts for weights and wire hooks. Even with such rude gear they caught a great number, but their recreation was suddenly terminated, a young man who was drawing in a fish having dropped upon the deck quite senseless and apparently dead. He was carried below and put into his berth, there to pass through the successive stages of the fever.

Tuesday, 13 July

We were again becalmed during the forenoon, but a breeze that soon become a gale arose about 1 p.m. and lasted until evening, being accompanied by thunder and lightning and followed by a heavy shower of rain. The clouds cleared away at sunset when we were within 10 or 12 miles of the eastern point of the island of Anticosti which, when the captain perceived, he gave the order to sheer off on the other tack. This island is particularly dangerous, being surrounded by sunken reefs. It is of considerable extent, being 130 miles in length from east to west and 30 miles across its greatest breadth. Its surface is low and level and covered with a pristine forest, through which prowls the bear undisturbed, except when hunted by Indians who periodically resort hither for that purpose.

The sterility of its soil offering no inducement to the white man, it is uninhabited except by the keepers of the lighthouses to which are attached small establishments for the purpose of affording relief to shipwrecked mariners. The name 'Anticosti' is probably a corruption of Natiscotee, which it is called by the aborigines. Cartier named it L'isle de L'Assumption.

Wednesday, 14 July

We had the bold headlands of Capes Gaspé and Rosier on our left and had entered the majestic river St Lawrence which here, through a mouth 90 miles in width, after a course of upwards of 2,000 miles, disgorges the accumulated waters of the great lakes swollen by the accession of hundreds of tributaries (some of them noble rivers) draining an almost boundless region.

The reports of the suffering in the hold were heart-rending. Simon and Jack were both taken ill.

Last night I was suddenly wakened by the captain shouting 'Get up! Get up and come on deck quickly!' Somewhat alarmed I obeyed the summons as speedily as possible and was well recompensed for the start by the magnificence of the glorious scene I beheld. The northern portion of the firmament was vividly illuminated with a clear though subdued light, while across it shot fiery meteors from different directions, now rushing against each other as if engaged in deadly warfare, again gliding about in wanton playfulness.

Disappearing for a while and leaving behind a faintly luminous trail, they would again burst forth upon their stage, lighted up by a sudden flash for the igneous performers. I watched with delight until the lustrous picture was finally enshrouded in darkness when I returned to bed.

There was birth on board this morning and two or three deaths were momentarily expected. The mate's account of the state of the hold was harrowing. It required the greatest coercion to enforce anything like cleanliness or decency and the head committee had no sinecure office. I spent the greater part of the day upon deck, admiring the numberless *jets d'eau* of the bottlenose whales that plunged about in the water. The poor mistress was greatly grieved about Jack and Simon and the captain was savage for lack of assistance.

Friday, 16 July

We were tacking about all day which, though tedious I enjoyed, as it afforded an opportunity of seeing both shores of the noble river. That to the north is indescribably grand, rugged mountains rising precipitously from out the water, and indented by sweeping bays, in which are numerous islets. Towards evening we were in view of Seven Islands Bay, lovely though desolate. No human eyes behold this region of unbroken solitude, save now and then those which can but lightly appreciate its grandeur. I cannot describe the effect produced by the mist that sometimes completely hides the mountains, rolling up their sides and resembling gracefully festooned drapery.

The sailors who could work were greatly harassed by being obliged to tack repeatedly. The mate especially was one moment down in the hold waiting on some dying fellow creature; the next perhaps stretched across a yard, reefing a top-sail. Although lame, he was surprisingly active and used to astonish the emigrants, one of whom said to me 'Och! your honour, isn't Mr Mate a great bit of a man?'

Saturday, 17 July

The morning was fine and shortly after breakfast I was upon deck admiring the beauty of the pine-clad hills upon the southern shore of the river, when the captain came up from the cabin and after looking about gave the word to 'double reef top-sail and make all snug'. Not long after, the sky, which had been quite clear, became black and a violent gale arose, lashing the water into tremendous waves which tossed us mercilessly about, one moment borne up by an angry billow, the next plunging into a deep abyss. The roaring wind was drowned by the tremendous noise of successive peals of thunder, while the forked lightning played about in zigzag lines and the rain descended in torrents.

At 5 p.m. the wind abated and the waves began to subside. About an hour after, the leaden clouds parted and, as if in defiance of the contending elements, the sun set in gorgeous splendour. The poor passengers were greatly terrified by the storm and suffered exceedingly. They were so buffeted about that the sick could not be tended and after calm was restored a woman was found dead in her berth.

Chapter VII

So frequent death,
Sorrow he more than causes, but confounds;
For human sighs, his rival strokes contend,
And make distress, distraction.

Young

Sunday, 18 July

I was enchanted with the extraordinary beauty of the scenery I beheld this morning when I came on deck. The early beams of the sun played upon the placid surface of the river, here 40 miles wide, the banks on either hand being moderately elevated and covered with firs. On the north was Cape des Monts, terminating in a low point on which stood a lighthouse and diminutive cottage. On the south Cape Chat rose to a considerable height, the outline of its summit being broken by sudden gaps, giving to it a character that to me was unique.

An unbroken stillness reigned around as if nature were at rest after the storm of the previous day and our brig lay almost motionless upon the water.

I occupied myself again and again noting, so as to impress upon my mind, the peerless beauty I am unable to portray and in reading the Acts of the Apostles. I felt a renewed interest in the account of St Paul's voyages as I could now appreciate by experience the force and accuracy of their description. We made no way and it was with difficulty we retained our position against the current.

Another death and burial. A few who had been ill again appeared on deck, weak and weary. The want of pure water was sensibly felt by the afflicted creatures and we were yet a long way from where the river loses its saltiness. In the morning there came alongside of us a beautiful little schooner, from which we took a pilot on board. When he found that we had emigrants and so much sickness he seemed to be frightened and disappointed as he had avoided a large ship, thinking we had not passengers. However, he could not dare

49

retreat. The first thing he did was to open his huge trunk and take from it a pamphlet which proved to be the quarantine regulations. He handed it to the captain who spent a long time poring over it. When he had read it I got a look at it, one side was printed in French, the other in English. The rules were very stringent and the penalties for their infringement exceedingly severe, the sole control being vested in the head physician, the power given to whom was most arbitrary. We feared that we should undergo a long detention in quarantine and learned that we could hold no communication whatever with the shore until our arrival at Grosse Isle.

The pilot was a heavy, stupid fellow, a Canadian, speaking a horrible patois and broken English. He was accompanied by his nephew and apprentice, Pierre – a fine lad,

The wind favoured us for some hours and towards evening we saw Mount Camille upon the southern bank, rising above the surrounding hills to a height of 2,036 feet.

Tuesday, 20 July

Our course lying more to the southern bank of the river, I could observe minutely the principal objects upon that side. Many charming tributary streams rolled along sweet valleys, enfolded in the swelling hills, whose sides were clothed with verdure. I would fain explore each of these enchanting vales but too soon we passed them and some jutting cape would hide from view the little settlements at each embouchure. The most considerable of these was that upon Point aux Snellez, near the mouth of the river Métis, about 200 miles from Quebec. Here commences the Kempt road which terminates at Cross Point on the river Restigouche, a distance of 98 miles. A new road, connecting this with Grande Nouvelle on the Bay des Chaleur, completes the communication with Halifax.

Wednesday, 21 July

A thick fog concealed every object from view, at times so low as only to hide the hulls of vessels by whose rigging we could perceive them tacking like ourselves, the sky being unclouded. A strong wind blew down the river, which, together with the forcible current kept us back. One of the sick sailors reappeared upon deck but was too weak to resume duty. The other man was still very bad as were also Simon and Jack.

Simon got up from his berth in a delirious fit and ran down to the cabin, where his wild appearance nearly frightened the life out of the mistress. It was with difficulty he was laid hold of and he resisted violently while he was carried back to his hammock in the forecastle where he was strapped down.

Thursday, 22 July

Soon after retiring to my berth last night I heard a grating noise accompanied by a tremulous motion of the brig and felt alarmed, fearing that we had grounded upon some bank, but my anxiety was relieved by learning that it was caused by the dropping of the anchor, it being useless to contend against both wind and current, the latter here being strengthened by the vast body of water discharged from the river Saguenay. When I came on deck this morning I found that we were anchored off the village of Trois Pistolles, with Cape L'Original to the east, and Basque Isle on the west. Being the first Canadian village I had seen, I was delighted by the rural aspect of the pretty white cottages with red roofs, scattered over the sloping bank, each surrounded by a small garden. The captain was impatient and though the pilot said it would only tend to harass the sailors, we weighed anchor at noon and, after beating about all the day, again came to, near the same spot as before. A child – one of the orphans – died and was buried in the evening, no friend being by to see the frail body committed to its watery grave. The water could not be used by the wretched emigrants and but half a cask of that provided for the cabin and crew remained. They were therefore obliged to use the saline water of the river.

We remained at anchor all day, a fresh breeze blowing down the river. Some of the recovered patients who were slowly regaining strength had relapsed into the most violent stages and three new cases were announced, showing exceedingly virulent symptoms.

The wind abated at noon and it was quite calm for about an hour. During this period I was up on deck and on looking across the river was greatly astonished at perceiving something resembling an island which I had not before noticed. It was circular and quite black. I spent some time in conjecturing what it could be. The captain could not tell and the pilot was asleep. At length, two vessels sailing down the river, when they came near this object, assumed a similar appearance – from which I immediately inferred that it was a ship at anchor, transformed by mirage.

As the vessels sailed along they underwent extraordinary metamorphoses – sometimes the bow and stern were turned up like those of a Chinese junk. At others the hulls were up in the air and the masts seemingly in the water; the latter being twisted and curved. A cottage upon the north bank stood apparently upon the surface of the river and the lighthouse on Bic Island had a duplicate of itself perched upon it, the copy being inverted, lantern down and base up. The illusions occurred only within certain limits which were defined by an appearance distinct from the surrounding atmosphere. The difference being something like that presented by clear water and the empty space within a half filled vial.

CHAPTER VIII

These are miracles, which men,
Cag'd in the bounds of Europe's pigmy plan,
Can scarcely dream of; which his eye must see,
To know how beautiful this world can be.

Moore

Saturday, 24 July

We once more weighed anchor this morning and beat about all the day between Trois Pistoles and the mouth of the river Escamin which discharges itself nearly opposite, upon the north shore. We had a large fleet of ships, barques and brigs in company, two of which were transports with troops. It was a pleasing sight to see such a number of vessels continually passing each other and each evidently endeavouring to gain upon the rest, every tack.

In the afternoon, a brig hoisted her ensign as a signal of recognition and upon the next tack we passed near enough to speak. When the captain turned out to be a particular friend of our captain and the mistress, they kept up a regular conversation the rest of the day every time we met, which was pretty often, each inquiring of the other: the number of deaths? what sickness? how many days out? from what port? etc. We learned – much to our surprise – that she had a greater number of deaths than we and this news was very consoling to the mistress. Towards evening the wind abated and we were in hope that it was about to change. It died away altogether and the vessels that before shot past one another were now almost motionless and scattered over the surface of the river, which here is 25 miles wide.

At sunset we lay at the north side and could almost reach the trees covering the bank. I have seen many a beautiful sunset but all fade before the exquisite beauty of that which I witnessed this evening. The glorious luminary sunk behind the dark blue hills upon the summits of which seemed to rest the border of heaven's canopy, dyed in crimson sheen, softening down to a light orange tint that imperceptibly blended with the azure sky, which was here and there hid by fleecy vermilion clouds. Cape L'Orignal was clothed in a vesture of purple of every shade from violet to that of the deepest hue, o'ershadowing the village of Trois Pistolles. There was not a ripple upon the water but gentle undulations heaved its bosom, decked in a tissue of carmine, ultramarine and gold. Such vividness and variety of colours I never before conceived or since experienced. Oh! thought I, why is not Danby here to fix them upon imperishable canvas? As night came on, the pilot grew uneasy, there not being good anchorage at that side. However, a slight breeze from the old quarter wafted us across to the very spot where we before lay and where we again dropped anchor in the midst of our consorts.

Sunday, 25 July

We lay at anchor all day, the wind blowing strongly against us. It was exceedingly trying to be detained here within a few miles of the tidal influence, having once gained which, we would be independent of the wind. The poor patients, too, were anxiously looking out for the quarantine station where they hoped to find some alleviation of their sufferings. The mistress and mate were uneasy, as the cabin water was nearly out and they feared to let the captain know of it.

I was obliged to remain below, the effluvia from the hold being quite overpowering. I could hear the tolling of the village church-bell and its sweet tone induced me to go on deck for a few moments where I was charmed with the appearance of the showily dressed Canadians, some standing in groups talking, others seated upon benches while *caleshes*

54

were momentarily arriving with *habitans* from distant settlements who, after tying up their horses under a shed close by the *presbytère*, joined the chatting parties until the bell ceased, when all retired within the church.

Monday, 26 July

The wind was not so strong and the effluvia not quite so unpleasant. I was therefore not so much confined to the cabin. The captain was desirous of sailing but the pilot would not consent and the latter proved to be right, as two of the vessels weighed anchor in the morning and after beating about for a couple of hours were obliged to come to. A pretty stream – the mingled waters of the Abawisquash and Trois Pistolles rivers – flows into the St Lawrence adjacent to the village. Like all the tributaries upon the southern side, it is of inconsiderable length, the hills in which they have their sources lying at no great distance from the bank. But many of those which empty themselves at the north side as the, Manicouagan, Bustard, Belsiamites, Portneuf, etc, are fine rivers rising in the elevated ridge that divides Canada from the Hudson's Bay territory and, in their courses through the untrodden forests, expanding into large lakes.

After dinner, the mistress carried down to the cabin the baby that was born on board. The captain at first was very angry but a smile upon the face of the little innocent softened his heart and he soon caressed it with all the endearments he was in the habit of lavishing upon the canary. When tired of which amusement, he opened the locker and took therefrom an egg, which he held up to the light and looked through to see if it were good. Not being satisfied on that point he tried another and then another, until he got one to please him. He next got some salt and, opening the infant's little hand, placed it upon the palm and gently closed the tiny fingers upon it. He then performed a similar operation upon the other, enclosing a shilling in lieu of salt. The egg he handed to the mistress to send to the mother and acquaint her that he wished the child to be called 'Ellen', after her.

The mistress, kind to all, was particularly so to the little children about twenty of whom we had aboard. One poor infant whose father and mother (neither of whom was twenty years of age) were both ill and unable to take care of it, she paid a woman for nursing and I could not believe it to be the same child when I saw it clean and comfortably covered with clothes she made for it.

Jack came upon deck. Poor fellow! he was sadly altered. Simon also was reported to be better but unable to leave his hammock. The mate began to complain and the brandy cask (which had been broached) supplied his remedy.

Tuesday, 27 July

The wind veered about 5 o'clock last evening and the vessels one by one sailed away. Our pilot, saying that it would again change in a short time, was not inclined to weigh anchor but the captain insisted upon doing so. At 6 p.m. we were once more in motion and in a few minutes were in full sail going 7 knots an hour. Basque Island was soon left behind and, stemming the dark waters discharged by the Saguenay, as day was fading, we were before Tadoussac, a settlement at the mouth of that grand river.

The Saguenay ranks second amongst the tributaries of the St Lawrence. Indeed, although its course is not so long it is supposed to convey a larger body of water than the Ottawa. At its juncture with the St Lawrence it is about a mile wide but in some parts it expands to three. At a distance of 140 miles it receives the waters of Lake St John which is the reservoir of numerous rivers, some of which are precipitated into it by magnificent rapids and falls. This lake, which is about 100 miles in circumference, is remarkable for its shallowness from which cause the navigation of it is frequently dangerous, as the least wind produces a ground swell and breakers. Its water is said to be tepid and it abounds with a variety of fish, great quantities of which are taken at the mouth of the Ouiatchouan river where there is a station at which they are salted and packed for traffic. The climate is very salubrious and the soil of the great valley that borders the lake is susceptible of the highest culture. A few Indians wander over this fine tract of country which it is the intention of the provincial government to open to French Canadians whose laws acknowledging no right of primogeniture, they have overpopulated many of the old settlements. The Indians call this fine sheet of water 'Piegongamis,' signifying 'the flat lake'. First-class ships can ascend the Saguenay to Chicoutimi, a distance of 68 miles. There is a small settlement here, the communication between which and the lake, being broken by rapids, can only be overcome by experienced *voyageurs* in canoes. At Ha-Ha Bay, 18 miles below Chicoutimi, there is a pretty large settlement and here the river assumes its grand and romantic feature, passing for the remainder of its course between almost perpendicular cliffs from 1,000 to 1,500 feet in height. Its great depth is another characteristic, bottom not being found near the mouth with a line of 330 fathoms, while the depth of the St Lawrence at the junction is but 240 feet. However, its great rapidity renders it impossible accurately to learn its soundings.

CHAPTER IX

But soft! the tinges of the west decline,
And night falls dewy o'er these banks of pine.
Among the reeds in which our idle host
Is rock'd to rest, the wind's complaining note
Dies like a half breath'd whispering of flutes.
Along the waves the gleaming porpoise shoots.
And I can trace him like a wat'ry star,
Down the steep current, till he fades afar
Amid the foaming breakers' silvery light,
Where you rough rapids sparkle through the night.

Moore

Tuesday, 27 July

Feeling somewhat excited by the sudden acceleration of our progress, I determined to remain on deck until the turn of the tide would compel us to come to an anchor. There was something also most enchanting in being wafted by both wind and tide at the rate of 10 knots an hour, watching the lights upon the different islands and the myriads of bright stars that studded the firmament and were reflected in the darkened surface of the broad river, which upon the north side was overshadowed by the mountainous banks, while the southern shore might be traced by a continuous line of flickering lamps within the cottages upon its border.

We soon left Green Island behind us, then Hare Island and Rivière du Loup, upon which is a large settlement with a population of about 1,500. There are some large sawmills here and a *portage* leading through Madawaska to the lower provinces. After passing The Pilgrims, a group of rocky islets, I went below and had not long turned in when I heard and felt the dropping of the anchor.

In the morning I found that we lay off Kamouraska which is charmingly situated in a rich district at the base of a chain of hills that rise behind the village and stretch far beyond it. This lovely spot, being one of the healthiest places in

Lower Canada, attracts many visitors during the summer season. It is also enriched by the fisheries established upon the numerous islands that lie immediately in front supplying abundance of shad, salmon, herrings, etc. Directly opposite upon the other side of the river is Murray Bay, into which flows the Malbaie River, upon whose banks reside the descendants of Wolfe's highlanders many of whom settled there after the campaign. The bay is environed by an amphitheatre of majestic hills cultivated to the very summits, their sloping sides being dotted over with comfortable abodes.

We weighed anchor at noon and gently glided through a scene of indescribable loveliness. The noble river here unbroken by islands presented a lake-like expanse bounded by the lofty Cap Diable and Goose Cape. Village succeeded village upon the south shore and the gigantic hills upon the north were adorned by sweet alpine cots surrounded by cleared patches of land, embosomed by the dark green pines. The weather was very warm and nature basked in uninterrupted sunshine.

Oh! what a contrast to this magic beauty was presented within our floating pest-house, not that matters were worse than they had been, there was rather an abatement in the violence of the fever and I perceived some faces that I with difficulty recognised, so changed were they since I saw them before their illness. Simon and Jack were both on deck, the former being deprived of memory and partially deranged in his mind. Poor fellow having the previous voyage fallen from the topsail yard and injured his head, his intellect was thereby impaired and the fever confirmed the insanity which had not left him when I quitted the brig some three weeks after.

Being now in fresh water the passengers were relieved of one calamity and the women who were able were busy washing. Two or three men were also similarly engaged, their wives being unable and we endeavoured to impress upon them the fact that the length of our detention in quarantine would greatly depend on the cleanliness of their persons and of the hold. There were still some very bad cases and the poor head committee was in great trouble about his wife who was dying. The mate still kept up being afraid of going to hospital but it was quite evident that he was very ill indeed.

We passed two steamers that were going down the river to tow up ships. We also had a Scotch brig, the *Delta*, in company.

At 6 p.m, the tide being on the ebb, we once more anchored opposite to the Isle aux Coudres which lies in front of St Paul's Bay. This beautiful island was so named by Cartier who found upon it a profusion of filberts. A smaller island lies inside of it, whose origin is thus accounted for in a manuscript belonging to the Jesuit college of Quebec which relates the effects of the earthquake felt throughout Canada in 1663:

> Near St Paul's Bay (fifty miles below Quebec on the north side) a mountain about a quarter of a league in circumference, situated on the shore of the St Lawrence, was precipitated into the river but, as if it had only made a plunge, it rose from the bottom and became a small island forming with the shore a convenient harbour, well sheltered from all winds.

The same authority says:

> Lower down the river towards Point Alouette an entire forest of considerable extent was loosened from the main bank and slid into the river St Lawrence where the trees took fresh root.

The rivers Du Gouffre and Des Marées empty themselves into St Paul's Bay flowing through luxuriant valleys intervening between the detached mountains.

Delightfully located upon an eminence on the south bank stands the village of St Anne at the head of a bay of the same name into which flows the river Ouelle. It is large and has a Catholic college and some handsome churches.

The surrounding country is highly cultivated, presenting

every feature of softness and beauty that can adorn a landscape.

The evening was a charming one, clear and still. The water smooth as a mirror in which gleamed the reflection of the tin covered roofs and spires that glittered in the rays of the setting sun while occasionally a huge snow-white porpoise rose above the surface, plunging again beneath the water which, closing, formed circles becoming larger and larger until the unwieldy creature again appeared and formed them anew. I remained on deck long after all had retired to rest and watched the grey twilight creeping over day until it was illumined by the pale moon which soon smiled upon one of earth's most beauteous pictures.

I retired to my berth and took a short repose which was broken shortly after midnight by the weighing of the anchor. As I wished not to lose the sight of the least part of the river (which I loved to look upon by night as well as by day) I hurried on deck.

We passed through the Traverse, an intricate channel, marked by floating lights and by the Pillars, a group of dangerous rocks on one of which is a revolving light. At daybreak we were passing Goose Island which at low water is connected with Crane Island on the northern extremity of which is the handsome residence of the seigneur. The southern bank presented the same charming features and in the distance I discerned the chain of hills claimed by the United States as the boundary of the State of Maine. In a short time we arrived before the village of St Thomas picturesquely situated on the banks of Rivière du Sud in which were anchored some vessels which were being freighted with lumber from the several saw-mills. The soil in this neighbourhood is exceedingly productive and is well cultivated – on which account it is called the granary of the lower province. The village is of considerable extent and is composed of white houses clustering around a pretty church.

A few miles further sail brought us among a number of

beautiful islets, so beautiful that they seemed like a fairy scene. Their verdant turf was almost level with the blue water that wound amongst them, submerging not a few so that the first that grew upon them appeared to rise from the river. A vast fleet of vessels lying at anchor told that we had arrived at Grosse Isle, and after wending our way amongst isles and ships, we dropped anchor in the ground allotted for vessels upon arrival and hoisted our ensign at the peak as a signal for the inspecting physician to board us.

CHAPTER X

And when I looked, behold, a hand was sent unto
me, and, lo, a roll of a book was therein:

And he spread it before me: and it was written
within and without: and there was written therein,
lamentations and mourning, and woe.

Ezekiel

Grosse Isle, Wednesday, 28 July

By 6 a.m. we were settled in our new position before the
quarantine station. The passengers that were able to be
up were all busy clearing and washing, some clearing
the hold of filth, others assisting the sailors in swabbing the
deck. The mistress herself washed out the cabin last evening
and put everything in order.

The captain commenced shaving himself at 7 and completed the operation in about an hour and a half. The mate
was unable to do anything but kept repeatedly calling to the
mistress for brandy and requested that his illness should be
kept from the doctor as he was sure he had not fever. Breakfast was speedily despatched and anxiety was depicted on
every countenance. At 9 o'clock a boat was perceived pulling
towards us with four oars and a steersman with broad-leafed
straw hat and leather coat who, the pilot told us, was the inspecting physician. In a few minutes the boat was alongside
and the doctor on deck. He hastily enquired for the captain
and before he could be answered was down in the cabin
where the mistress was finishing her toilet. Having introduced himself he enquired: if we had sickness aboard? Its nature? How many patients at present? These questions being
answered and the replies noted upon his table, he snatched
up his hat ran up the ladder along the deck and down into
the hold.

Arrived there, 'Ha!' said he sagaciously, 'there is fever

here.' He stopped beside the first berth in which a patient was lying, felt his pulse, examined his tongue and ran up the ladder again. As he passed by me he handed me some papers to be filled up by the captain and to have ready 'tomorrow or next day'. In an instant he was in his boat from which, while the men were taking up their oars, he shouted out to me that I was not obliged to remain in quarantine and might go up to Quebec when I pleased.

I brought the papers to the captain who remained in the cabin, supposing that the doctor would return thither, in order to give directions for our guidance, and when he learned that that gentleman had gone, he was desperately enraged. The mistress endeavoured to pacify him by suggesting that it was likely he would visit us again in the course of the day or at least that he would send a message to us. When I acquainted the mistress that I was at liberty to leave the brig she looked at me most pitifully as if she would say, 'Are you too going to desert us?' But I had no such intention and was determined to remain with them at all events until they reached Quebec.

The poor passengers, expecting that they would be all reviewed, were dressed in their best clothes and were clean, though haggard and weak. They were greatly disappointed in their expectations as they were under the impression that the sick would be immediately admitted to the hospital and the healthy landed upon the island, there to remain until taken to Quebec by a steamer. Indeed, such was the procedure to be inferred from the book of directions given to the captain by the pilot when he came aboard.

When the mistress appeared on deck I scarcely knew her. She usually wore a black stuff gown, a red worsted 'bosom friend', which she told me (at least once a day) was knit for her by her niece, with a cap, having three full borders which projected beyond the leaf of the little straw bonnet, covered with the accumulated stains and smoke of many a voyage. Now she had on a new fancy striped calico dress as showy as deep reds, yellows, blues and greens could make it; a black satin bonnet with no lack of red ribands and a little conservatory of artificials around her good-natured face, not forgetting her silver spectacles. All day long we kept looking out for a message from shore and in watching the doctor's boat going from vessel to vessel. His visit to each occupying about the same as to us – which was exactly five minutes. We sometimes fancied that he was making for us but the boat the next moment would be concealed by some large ship. Then we were sure we would be the next – but no, the rowers poled for shore. The day wore away before we gave up hope.

I could not believe it possible that here, within reach of help, we should be left as neglected as when upon the ocean. That after a voyage of two months' duration we were to be left still enveloped by reeking pestilence, the sick without medicine, medical skill, nourishment or so much as a drop of pure water – for the river, although not saline here, was polluted by the most disgusting objects thrown overboard from the several vessels. In short, it was a floating mass of filthy straw, the refuse of foul beds, barrels containing the vilest matter, old rags and tattered clothes, etc.

The head committee was greatly grieved for his wife whose death he momentarily expected. He had looked anxiously forward to the time when we should arrive here, hoping that at least the doctor would see her, but his hopes – as well as those of others – were suddenly blasted. The brig that arrived with us sailed for Quebec immediately after the doctor's visit, possibly not having had any sickness. Five other vessels also were discharged. How long they were detained we could not tell but the captain was so provoked that he vowed he would sail without permission. The pilot, who did not well understand his hasty disposition, ventured to remonstrate with him and fell in for a hurricane of curses and abuse to which, though ignorant of many of the expressions, he replied in French, not finding himself sufficiently eloquent in the English tongue.

Four vessels arrived with the evening tide and hoisted their signals but were not visited. Several sailed by us without stopping, not having passengers, and a vast number went down the river during the day.

Two huge steamers also arrived and in the afternoon brought off hundreds of human beings from the island.

Thursday, 29 July

This morning, a boat was perceived making towards us which at first was thought to be the doctor's but when it approached nearer there appeared but two persons in it, both of whom were rowing. In a few minutes more the boat was alongside and from the cassocks and bands of the two gentlemen we learned that they were Canadian priests. They came on deck, each carrying a large black bag. They inquired for the captain who received them courteously and introduced them to the mistress and to me, after which they conversed a while in French with the pilot whom they knew. When having put on their vestments, they descended into the hold. They there spent a few minutes with each of the sick and administered the last rites to the dying woman and an old man, terminating their duties by baptising the infant. They remained in the hold for about an hour and, when they returned, complimented the captain on the cleanliness of the vessel.

They stayed a short time talking to us upon deck and the account they gave of the horrid condition of many of the ships in quarantine was frightful. In the holds of some of them they said that they were up to their ankles in filth. The wretched emigrants crowded together like cattle and corpses remaining long unburied – the sailors being ill and the passengers unwilling to touch them. They also told us of the vast numbers of sick in the hospitals and in tents upon the island and that many nuns, clergymen and doctors were lying in typhus fever, taken from the patients.

They were exceedingly intelligent and gentlemanly men and, telling us that we had great case of thankfulness in having escaped much better than so many others, they politely bowed and got into their little boat, amid the blessings of the passengers who watched them until they arrived beside a distant ship.

The head committee expressed himself satisfied that his wife saw a priest before her death which occurred about an hour after, and as the pilot said that the remains should not be thrown into the river – there being a burial ground upon the island – the corpse lay in the hold until the next day.

The mate continued to grow worse and the mistress was unceasing in her attention to him. The day was exceedingly hot and sultry and I could not have remained on deck but the captain spread an awning over it which kept the cabin cool. We lay at some distance from the island, the distant view of which was exceedingly beautiful. At the far end were rows of white tents and marquees, resembling the encampment of an army. Somewhat nearer was the little fort and residence of the superintendent physician and nearer still the chapel, seaman's hospital and little village with its wharf and a few sail boats, the most adjacent extremity being rugged rocks, among which grew beautiful fir trees. At high water this portion was detached from the main island and formed a most picturesque islet.

However, this scene of natural beauty was sadly deformed by the dismal display of human suffering that it presented – helpless creatures being carried by sailors over the rocks on their way to the hospital, boats arriving with patients some of whom died in their transmission from their ships. Another, and still more awful sight, was a continuous line of boats, each carrying its freight of dead to the burial ground and forming an endless funeral procession. Some had several corpses so tied up in canvas that the stiff, sharp outline of death was easily traceable. Others had rude coffins constructed by the sailors from the boards of their berths, or I should rather say, cribs. In a few, a solitary mourner attended the remains but the majority contained no living beings save the rowers. I would not remove my eyes until boat after boat was hid by the projecting point of the island, round which they steered their gloomy way. From one ship a boat proceeded four times during the day, each time laden with a cargo of dead. I ventured to count the number of boats that passed but had to give up the sickening task.

The inspecting doctor went about from vessel to vessel, six of which came in each tide and as many sailed. We expected him to visit us every moment but he did not come near us.

In the afternoon a boat made for our brig and the mistress, who was on deck, was greatly delighted to find that it contained two 'captains', one of whom was her nephew. One arrived the day before we came, the other a day previous. They were as ignorant of the course of proceeding as we and before they went away it was agreed on that they, our captain and I should wait on the superintendent physician the next day.

CHAPTER XI

As from the wing no scar the sky retains,
The parted wave no farrow from the keel,
So dies in human hearts the thought of death.
E'en with the tears which nature shed
O'er those we love, we drop it in their graves.
Young

Friday, 30 July

This morning when I came on deck, a sailor was busily employed constructing a coffin for the remains of the head committee's wife and it was afflicting to bear the husband's groans and sobs accompanying each sound of the saw and hammer, while, with his motherless infant in his arms, he looked on. About an hour after, the boat was lowered and the bereaved husband, with four rowers, proceeded to the burial ground to inter the corpse, and they were followed by many a tearful eye until the boat disappeared behind the rocky point.

At 10 a.m. we descried the doctor making for us, his boatmen pulling lustily through the heavy sea. A few minutes brought him alongside and on board, when he ran down to the cabin and demanded: if the papers were filled up with a return of the number of deaths at sea? How many cases of sickness? etc. He was handed them by the captain, when he enquired how many patients we then had. He was told there were twelve, when he wrote an order to admit six to hospital, saying that the rest should be admitted when there was room – there being 2,500 at that time upon the island and hundreds lying in the various vessels before it. The order written, he returned to his boat and then boarded a ship lying close to us, which lowered her signal when he approached. Several other vessels that arrived in the morning had their ensigns flying at the peak until each was visited in turn.

Immediately after the doctor left us, the captain gave orders to have the patients in readiness. Shortly after, our second boat was launched and four of the passengers volunteered to row – the sailors that were able to work, being with the other. O God! May I never again witness such a scene as that which followed: the husband, the only support of an emaciated wife and helpless family, torn away forcibly from them in a strange land; the mother dragged from her orphan children that clung to her until she was lifted over the bulwarks, rending the air with their shrieks; children snatched from their bereaved parents who were perhaps ever to remain ignorant of their recovery, or death. The screams pierced my brain and the excessive agony so rent my heart that I was obliged to retire to the cabin where the mistress sat weeping bitterly.

The captain went in the boat and returned in about an hour, giving us a frightful account of what he witnessed upon the island.

The steamers returned and all the afternoon were engaged taking the healthy passengers out of some of the vessels. They went alongside several until their cargo was complete when they sailed for Montreal, their decks thickly crowded with human beings and – most extraordinary to relate – each of them had a fiddler and a dancing party in the prow.

Early in the evening the captain's nephew came to take us in his boat, on shore. After a long pull through a heavy swell, we landed upon the Isle of Pestilence and, climbing over the rocks, passed through the little town and by the hospitals, behind which were piles upon piles of unsightly coffins. A little further on, at the edge of a beautiful sandy beach, were several tents, into one of which I looked but had no desire to see the interior of any others. We pursued our way by a road cut through a romantic grove of firs, birch, beech and ash, beneath the shade of which grew and blossomed charming wild flowers, while the most curious fungi vegetated upon odd, decayed stumps. The path led us into a cleared lawn, passing through which we arrived in front of the superintendent physician's cottage, placed upon a sloping bank at the river's side, on which were mounted two pieces of ordnance guarded by a sentinel. The view from this spot was exquisitely beautiful; upon the distant bank of the broad river were the smiling, happy-looking Canadian villages backed by deep blue hills, while the agitated water in front tossed the noble vessels that lay at anchor and which were being swung round by the turning tide.

The doctor not being within, we walked about until his return when he invited us into his cottage and heard what the captains had to say, after which he promised to discharge our friend the next day and that he would send a steamer to take our passengers. He also gave the captain an order for the admission of the mate to the seaman's hospital. Our mission having been so successful, we thanked the doctor and departed. Upon our return we called at the store licensed to sell provisions upon the island. It was well stocked with various commodities among which were carrion beef and cattish mutton, bread, flour, cheese, etc. Although the captain wished to treat the mistress to fresh meat, he declined purchasing what we saw and merely bought some flour. The storekeeper did not lack better customers, however, for there was a vast concourse of mates, stewards, seamen and boys buying his different articles and stowing them away in their boats. The demand for bread was very great and several batches were yielded from a large oven while we remained.

Hearing the music of a fiddle accompanied by the stamping of feet in time with the tune, I walked up to the shed from which it issued. There were two men dancing a jig, one of them a Canadian, the other a sailor – both fine fellows who were evidently pitted against each other in a trial of skill. The former wore huge boots coming above the knees and, drawn over his grey trousers composed of *étoffe du pays*, a light blue flannel shirt confined at the waist by a scarlet

71

scarf whose particoloured ends hung at one side. On his head was a woollen *bonnet rouge* whose tassel jumped about with the wearer's movements. His brilliant black eyes lighted up his swallow visage and his arms were as busily engaged as his legs. The sailor was rigged out in pumps, white trousers, blue jacket and straw hat with streaming black ribands, his ruddy face glowing with the exercise. The fiddler's costume was similar to that of his brother Canadian except that his bonnet was blue. He stood upon a barrel and around the dancers was a circle of *habitans* and sailors who encouraged them by repeated 'bravo's'. I did not remain long nor could I enjoy the amusement in such a place and therefore joined my companions in the boat where we were detained a few moments while one of the men returned for lime which the captain had forgotten to procure. He soon returned and, again ploughing through the waves, we shortly arrived beneath the *Leander*, after examining which noble ship, the captain and I returned to the brig and acquainted the mistress with the issue of our adventure.

Our boat returned just at the same time, the men having been away all the day. It appeared that they could not find the burial ground and consequently dug a grave upon an island when as they were depositing the remains they were discovered and obliged to decamp. They were returning to the brig when they perceived several boats proceeding in another direction and, having joined them, were conducted to the right place. The wretched husband was a very picture of desperation and misery that increased the ugliness of his countenance, for he was sadly disfigured by the marks of small pox and was blind of an eye. He walked moodily along the deck, snatched his child from a woman's arms and went down into the hold without speaking a word. Shortly after, one of the sailors who was with the boat told me that after the grave was filled up he took the shovels and placing them cross-wise upon it, calling heaven to witness said, 'By that cross, Mary, I swear to revenge your death – as soon as I earn the price of my passage home, I'll go back and shoot the man that murdered you and that's the landlord.'

It was with great reluctance that the mate consented to go to hospital, and as he went into the boat he charged the captain, the mistress and me with cruelty. The captain went with him and gave him in charge of a doctor.

In consequence of the superintendent's promise to send a steamer to take our passengers and give us clean bills if the vessel were well whitewashed between decks, the passengers' berths were all knocked away and the filthy boards thrown into the river, after which four men worked away cleaning and whitening all the day – but no steamer arrived that day. One which lay overnight took 250 passengers from the captain's nephew who sailed not long after.

Vessels were arriving with every tide; two ships from Bremen came in the morning and were discharged at once, having no sickness. Some others sailed up with the evening tide, after which there were more than 30 in quarantine. Boats were plying all day long between the several vessels and the island and, the sea being high, the miserable patients were drenched by the spray, after which they had to clamber over the slimy rocks or were carried by sailors. There was also an almost unbroken line of boats carrying the dead for interment. Then there was the doctor's boat, unceasingly shooting about, besides several others containing captains of ships, many of whom had handsome gigs with six oars and uniformly dressed rowers. It was indeed a busy scene of life and death. To complete the picture, the rigging of the vessels was covered over with the passengers' linen hanging out to dry – by the character of which as they fluttered in the breeze, I could tell with accuracy from what country they came; alas! the wretched rags of the majority told but too plainly that they were Irish.

CHAPTER XII

O the tender ties,
Close twisted with the fibres of the heart,
Which broken break them, and drain off the soul
Of human joy; and make it pain to live.

Young

Sunday, 1 August

The passengers passed a miserable night, huddled up as they were without room to stretch their weary limbs. I pitied them from my soul and it was sickening to see them drink the filthy water. I could not refuse to give one or two of them a mouthful from the cask upon the quarter deck which fortunately was filled lower down the river. They asked for it so pitifully and were so thankful – but I could not satisfy all and regretted the disappointment of many.

They had on their best clothes and were all clean, with the exception of one incorrigible family. The doctor came on board in the forenoon to inspect the passengers, who were all called on deck but those who were unable. Placing himself at a barrier, he allowed each to pass, one by one, making those he suspected of being feverish show their tongues. This proceeding lasted about a quarter of an hour when the doctor went into the hold to examine those below and to see if it were clean. He then wrote out the order to admit the six patients to hospital and promised to send the steamer to take the remainder, after which we should have clean bills. When he had gone, the patients were lowered into the boat amid a renewal of the indescribable woe that followed the previous separations. Two of them were orphan sisters who were sent for by a brother in Upper Canada. Another was a mother who had tended all her family through illness, now careworn and heart-broken, she became herself a prey.

In the early part of the voyage I observed the unfilial conduct of a boy who frequently abused and even cursed his mother, following the example set by his wretched father. On one occasion his hand was raised to strike her when his arm was arrested by a bystander, but the poor woman begged of the man not to punish him and wept for the depravity of her son. It was she who was now being carried to the boat while the boy who cursed and would have stricken her, clung to her, crying and imploring her blessing and forgiveness but she was unable to utter a word and, by an effort, raised her arm feebly and looked sadly upon the afflicted boy who seized her hand and bathed it with his tears until he was torn away and she dropped into the boat which, a moment after, rowed off. I felt much for the poor fellow who was conscious that he should never again see his mother for there was no hope of her recovery and I little thought that any one could be so heartless as to aggravate his sufferings as did two or three women who surrounded him, one of them saying, 'Ha! You villain there's the mother you abused and cursed, you rascal! You may now take your last look at her.' He followed the boat with his eyes until it reached the shore when he beheld the inanimate figure borne to the hospital. It was evident from the poignancy of his sorrow that his heart was not depraved but that his conduct arose from education.

The morning was fine, clear and warm and many of the vessels were decorated with their flags giving a cheerful aspect to the scene which, alas, was marred by the ensigns of two ships (one on either side of us) which were hoisted half-mast high, the captain of one and the chief mate of the other, being dead. While the captain was away with the boat, the steamer came alongside of us to take our passengers. It did not take very long to transship them as few of them had any luggage. Many of them were sadly disappointed when they learned that they were to be carried on to Montreal, as those who had left their relatives upon Grosse Isle hoped that, as

Quebec was not far distant, they would be enabled by some means to hear of them by staying there. Each of them shook hands with the mistress and all heaped blessings upon her head and as to the captain, one of them remarked that, 'though he was a divil, he was a gintleman'.

The steamer pushed off amid the cheers of her motley freight and was soon out of sight. The mistress was quite overcome by the expressions of the poor creatures' gratitude for her unceasing and otherwise unrequited attention and benevolence. The captain returned and after dinner he and I went ashore for our clean bills of health. We saw Dr Douglas who informed us that the inspecting physician, Dr Jaques, had them and that he was going his rounds among the vessels with the intention of calling at the brig. But as we considered that it would probably be late before he would reach her, we pulled for a barque, beside which we descried the well-known boat. Before we were half way, it was gone and making for a ship some distance off; however, we still followed and again were disappointed. We determined not to give up the chase and at length caught the doctor on board a German emigrant vessel. He was inspecting the passengers of whom there were 500, all of them (without a single exception) comfortably and neatly clad, clean and happy. There was no sickness amongst them and each comely fair-haired girl laughed as she passed the doctor to join the group of robust young men who had undergone the ordeal.

Although it was pleasing to see so many joyous beings, it made me sad when I thought of the very, very different state of my unfortunate compatriots and I had become so habituated to misery, disease and death that the happiness that now surrounded me was quite discordant with my feelings. The doctor, having completed his task, countersigned our clean bills and handed them to the captain; we therefore thanked him and took our leave.

Before returning to the brig, we called to see the mate who was lying with his clothes on upon a bed, the next one to which contained a figure writhing in torture and, as the face was turned towards me, I recognised to my great surprise and dismay, the sailor who, but the evening but one before was dancing with the Canadian. When the mate perceived us he rose from the bed and, taking the captain by one arm and me by the other, walked us both out of the hospital to the porch saying that we had no business there as there was fever upon all sides of us. The hospital was a large chapel transformed to its present use and was exceedingly clean and well ventilated; the large windows were all open, causing a draught of air that was agreeable, the evening being very sultry.

We did not remain long with the mate who raved considerably in his conversation, though he said he was quite well. So, the captain giving him in charge of the attendant, with pressing injunctions to have every attention paid to him and saying that he hoped he would be able to join the brig upon his return, we departed. As we got into the boat we made a signal to the pilot (who was desired to be on the lookout) to weigh anchor so as not to lose the tide by any unnecessary delay. As we repassed the German ship, the deck was covered with emigrants who were singing a charming hymn, in whose beautiful harmony all took part, spreading the music of their 500 voices upon the calm, still air that wafted it around. The vessel being discharged began to move almost imperceptibly so that we quickly passed her but she gradually gained speed and was ahead of us by the time we reached the brig, and as the distance between us increased, the anthem died away until it became inaudible. It was the finest chorus I ever heard, performed in a theatre of unrivalled magnificence.

The mistress was delighted when she learned that we were free and all were glad to leave behind the Isle of Death, though we regretted leaving the mate there. The sailors that had been ill, still continuing very weak, the captain induced two young men to remain in order to assist in working the vessel. At 7 p.m. the anchor was weighed, the sails unreefed and we glided slowly along.

Chapter XIII

Sail on, sail on, thou fearless bark,
    Wherever blows the welcome wind;
It cannot lead to scenes more dark,
    More sad than those we leave behind.

Moore

It was indeed with gratefulness to the Almighty for having preserved me scatheless in the midst of the dread pestilence that I left Grosse Isle, and a more beautiful panorama I never beheld than the country through which we passed – the churches of St Thomas and St Pierre's, surrounded by handsome cottages and beautiful fields. On our right, Isle Madame, the largest of the numerous islands that clustered in the centre of the river, embosomed in the mighty steam beyond which rose Cap Tourment with the village of St Joachim at its base. And Mount St Anne, sheltering its village also – both of these lofty hills being of a deep purple hue. At sunset, we had reached the eastern extremity of the Isle of Orleans and an hour after, dropped anchor before St François, a sweet village composed of quaint looking cottages whose walls were as white as snow with red roofs, bright yellow doors and green venetian window blinds. Such was the universal style, all of them appearing as if they had been newly painted.

We again set sail soon after daybreak this morning with a breeze against us which compelled us to tack about. I did not regret this as I had many near views of the southern bank of the river and of the beautiful shore of Orléans Island with its luxuriant orchards and well cultivated farms flopping down to the water's edge, and dark forest upon the crest of its elevated interior. This fine island, which is 20 miles in length and 5 in width, is divided into five parishes and has a population of 5,000 Canadians. While it is an object

of the greatest beauty, it is at the same time of great useful-
ness – affording shelter to the harbour of Quebec on the east
side and producing large supplies of fruits and vegetables of
the finest description. The northern shore consists of low and
marshy beaches that abound with game. It is surprising that
there is no regular communication between the island and
the city during the summer season, but in winter it is easy of
access over the frozen river when the inhabitants convey
their produce to market. When Cartier visited it in the year
1535, the island was covered with vines, on which account
he called it the Isle of Bacchus. It was on it also that Wolfe
took up his quarters previous to the attack upon Quebec. At
8 a.m. we passed St Vallier and St John's; the latter upon the
island consisting of entirely white cottages which are chiefly
inhabited by the branch pilots upwards of 250 of whom find
lucrative employment in the river navigation during the
season, enabling them and their families to live comfortably
through the long winter in which they are unemployed.

At noon, we dropped anchor again before St Michel's,
where we lay until 6 p.m. when we once more renewed our
tacks, passing the sheltered cove called Patrick's hole, in
which a fine ship rode previous to leaving port for sea.

This little natural harbour is very valuable as it securely
shelters vessels that arrive before the winter's ice is sufficiently broken up to allow them to gain the city.

At Anseau Maraud which is adjacent, there were launched, in the year 1824, two enormous ships – the *Columbus* and
the *Baron of Renfrew* – which were built with the intention of
being broken up in England, the projectors thinking thereby
to save the duty on the timber of which they were constructed. But their object was frustrated by the decision that
a voyage should previously be made out of an English port.

The *Columbus* traversed the Atlantic and returned in
safety but was wrecked upon her second voyage. The *Baron*,
in whose construction 6,000 tons of timber were consumed,
was 309 feet long and of proportionate breadth. She sailed

for London on 25 August 1825 with a cargo (it is said of 10,000 tons) of lumber, her four masts crowded with sails, and followed down the river by a fleet of steamers and pleasure yachts. After a voyage of 50 days she arrived at Dover where she took on board both deal and river pilots but, her draft of water being 30 feet, she could not be taken through the queen's channel which is safe for ships of war. She was therefore obliged to remain outside of the Goodwin sands, near the entrance of the king's channel. Having encountered a violent gale, she grounded upon the Long sands but was got off on the following day. She safely rode out a second gale upon 19 October but successive storms and strong northerly winds eventually drove her upon the Flemish banks and, after being buffeted for several weeks by the waves, she was shattered to atoms; the fragments of the wreck and her cargo being wafted along the coast from Calais to Ostend.

Such was the history of these monster ships whose ill fortune deterred Canadian builders from again constructing such unwieldy vessels.

We next passed Beaumont where the south bank becomes elevated, increasing in height to Point Levi, the tin spire of whose church was visible, and on Orléans Island, St Famille.

The magnificent fall of Montmorenci then was revealed to view, in a sheet of tumbling snow-white foam, set between the dark green banks covered with fir and other trees. As we approached nearer, the low thundering sound of the 'many waters' broke on the ear, which died away as we sailed upon the other tack, and night spread its curtain over the splendid picture when we reached the mouth of the St Charles River where we dropped anchor.

I was charmed with the splendid prospect I enjoyed this morning when I came on deck.

The harbour was thickly covered with vessels, many of them noble ships of the largest class.

The city upon the side of Cape Diamond, with its tin-covered dome and spires sparkling in the morning sun and surrounded by its walls and batteries bristling with cannon, was crowned by the impregnable citadel, while a line of villages spread along the northern shore reaching to Beauport and Montmorenci. The lofty Mount St Anne bounding the view upon the east. Opposite the city lay Point Levi with the village of D'Aubigné. Crossing the river were steam ferry-boats, horse-boats and canoes and up the stream, far as the eye could reach, the banks were lined by wharves and timber ponds while the breeze wafted along a fleet of *bateaux* with great white sails, and numberless pilot boats were in constant motion.

We could not go ashore, neither dare any one come on board until we were discharged from quarantine by the harbour master and medical inspector. These functionaries approached us in a long six-oared boat with the Union Jack flying in her stern. When they came on board they demanded the ship's papers and clean bills of health which the captain gave them, in return for which he received a release from quarantine. Soon after they left us, a butcher brought us fresh meat, milk, eggs and vegetables to which we did ample justice at breakfast, when I went with the captain on shore.

I remained with the brig during her stay in Quebec harbour and sailed in her for Montreal on the evening of Thursday, 5 August. We were towed up the river by a steamboat and by daylight the following morning were passing the mouth of the river Batiscan.

The sail during the day was extremely pleasing; true the

82

St Lawrence did not present the same grand features as below Quebec but there was something of exceeding interest or beauty to be seen every moment. The banks varied in height but did not gain any great elevation and were lined by an almost unbroken chain of settlements, with villages upon either side at intervals of about 10 miles. At noon we sailed by Trois Rivières upon the River St Maurice which divides into three branches before it empties itself into the St Lawrence, forming two pretty islands connected with each other and the mainland by three handsome bridges. A couple of hours brought us into Lake St Peter which is an extension of the river and of intricate navigation, affording but a narrow channel which is marked out by buoys and beacons. Towards its western extremity it is full of low, marshy islands surrounded by rushes, between which lies the winding passage. At sunset we had a charming view of Sorel upon the eastern bank of the Richelieu which discharges the waters of lakes George and Champlain.

The river again narrowed and presented similar features as below the expansion. We anchored for the night and early next morning were forcing our way through the rapids called current St Mary, passing the village of Longueil and the charming isle St Helens. Montreal then opened to our view, and by 8 a.m. we were moored to its fine quay.

The brig, having completed her cargo, sailed for London on 19 August when I bade the captain and the mistress adieu and followed them some distance down the river until the favourable breeze that filled her sails wafted the brig out of sight.

I have represented these worthy people just as they appeared to me, and if I have spoken too plainly, I would crave their pardon should they ever recognise their lineaments in these sheets (which I do not think probable). Indeed, I should much regret causing their displeasure, having received from them every attention, their conduct towards me extending even to unwonted kindness and for which I shall never cease to feel grateful.

I was anxious to learn if the mate recovered and, in compliance with my desire, the captain wrote to me from Quebec and also from Green Island. The first of these letters was dated 23 August, and the following is an extract from it:

I got doun hear on satterday and saled all the way down which was a great saving to me it was bubful sale we Ankered all night and saled in the day which gave hus opertunety of seeing every Curisity we went on Shore and got Eags and milk and sead a little of the Contry this Mornning I am gowing on Shore if there be any Letters for you I will forward them to you I have not heard of my Mate Ariving hear yet which Disapoints me Greatly I wish you had bean with hus Yeasterday we had a Drive in the Countrey 9 Miles which was a plesent drive and toke tea in the Countrey a long with Cpt ---. I will sale on Tuesday Morning My Wife Joyns me in Cinde Regards to you.

In justice I must also quote the postscript: 'you must Excuse this as I am in a hury'.

The second letter was written on 27 August. In it the captain says:

I am sorey to inform you of my Mate being so hill I coled at Gruss Ile for him and went on shore and it would have hurt you much to have sean him he was mostly but a Skellitan but though as hill as he was, I should have brought him on Boord if the Docter would Aload me, I have not any hopes of him, he got nerely well, and mite have come up to the ship but as I told you made two frea with is self putting Bottel to is head Docter to my Wife and we are all well at present which I hope you cape you Helth, my Wife Joyns me in Cind regards to you.

I learned with satisfaction that the brig arrived at her destination in safety, but of the mate's fate I still remain ignorant. Of the passengers I never afterwards saw but two, both of them young men who got employment upon the Lachine Canal. The rest wandered over the country, carrying nothing with them but disease, and that but few of them survived the severity of the succeeding winter (ruined as their constitutions were) I am quite confident.

CHAPTER XIV

Of comfort not man speak.
Let's talk of graves, of worms and epitaphs;
Make dust our paper, and with rainy eyes
Write sorrow on the bosom of the earth.
Let's choose executors and talk of walls
And yet not so – for what can we bequeath,
Save our deposed bodies to the ground.

Shakespeare

That the system of quarantine pursued at Grosse Isle afforded but a very slight protection to the people of Canada is too evident from the awful amount of sickness and the vast number of deaths that occurred amongst them during the navigable season of 1847. From the plan that was adopted of sending the majority of the emigrants from the island directly up to Montreal, Quebec did not suffer so much as that city. However, during the three days I was there in the month of August too many signs of death were visible and upon a second and more prolonged visit, later in the season, it presented an aspect of universal gloom – the churches being hung in mourning, the citizens clothed in weeds and the newspapers recording daily deaths by fever contracted from the emigrants. To their honour and praise be it spoken, these alarming consequences did not deter either clergymen or physicians from the most unremitting zeal in performing their duty, and it is to be lamented that so many valuable lives were sacrificed. A paper of the month of September contained the following paragraph:

QUARANTINE STATION, GROSSE ISLE.
The Rev. J. Butler, missionary at Kingsey, went down on Tuesday morning to make his turn in attendance upon the sick at the quarantine station.

The Rev. Richard Anderson and Rev. N. Gueront came up on the evening of the same day. The former felt indisposed and thought it prudent to remain in town for the benefit of medical advice. If he should have an attack of fever the precaution thus early taken will, it is hoped, prevent its proving severe. We regret to say that the Rev. C.J. Morris recently returned from the station, is now seriously ill with Typhus Fever.

The death of the last gentleman is recorded as follows:

Died this morning at the private hospital at Beauport of typhus fever, the Rev. Charles J. Morris, A.M. missionary of the Church of England, at Portneuf in this district. Mr Morris contracted the disease which has thus proved fatal to him, in his ministrations to the sick at Grosse Isle. The funeral will take place in the Cathedral church, tomorrow afternoon, at 3 o'clock.

The Rev. Mr Anderson also died within a few days of the same period, and that the mortality continued to a late part of the season appears by the following from the *Boston Journal* of 1 December:

We learn from Quebec that Drs Painchaud and Jackson and seven or eight nuns of the Hôtel Dieu were sick with the ship fever. One of the Quebec physicians says that mortality among the physicians during the past season has been greater than it was during the Cholera.

On Sunday, 10 October, I had the pleasure of listening to a discourse delivered in St Patrick's chapel by Rev. Mr McMahon before he commenced which he read a list of the names of several persons (emigrants) who were separated from their families and who took this method of endeavouring to find them out. The Rev. gentleman also acknowledged having received several sums of money remitted from parties in Ireland to friends in Canada, amongst which he said were some without signatures, and one of these was directed 'To my Aunt Biddy', upon which his Reverence remarked that people should be more particular where money was concerned.

Although (as I have already stated) the great body of emigrants were sent out to Montreal by steamers, all of them could not be so transferred and many were detained in Quebec where the Marine and Emigrant Hospital contained during the season several hundreds – the number that remained upon 2 October being 113, of whom 93 were admitted during the week previous, and in which time there were discharged 132 and 46 died.

One of the first objects that appeared to my view upon my arrival in Montreal was the Emigrant Hospital upon Point St Charles, a low tract of ground cut off from the city by the Lachine Canal and on which the Indians were in the habit of encamping every summer before it was turned to its present purpose. On the day I arrived, 7 August, it contained 907 patients, 16 having died during the last 21 hours. An official return of burials in the city was furnished up to the same day, by which it appeared that during the previous nine weeks the number was 1,730, of which 924 were residents and 806 were emigrants. Exclusive of these, there died in the sheds 1,519 emigrants making a total of 3,240 – being 2,752 more than occurred during the corresponding period of the preceding year. Upon 23 August, the emigrant sheds contained 1,330 – 27 having died during twenty-four hours – and so late as 11 October, there remained 746 patients in them.

Montreal lost many of her most valuable citizens in consequence of the contagion, among whom were Dr Cushing and the mayor. Neither was the pestilence stayed here, for the inhabitants of Kingston, Bytown, Toronto and other places were infected and a great number died of the fever, amongst whom was the Rev. Dr Power, RC Bishop of Toronto who contracted the disease in the discharge of his sacred functions among the sick. The following extract taken from the *Toronto Standard* serves to the manner in which the people of Canada suffered, and their sympathy for those who brought so much woe amongst them:

> The health of the city remains in much the same state as it did several weeks ago. The individual cases of fever have abated nothing of their violence and several families have caught the

infection from having admitted emigrants into their houses. The greatest caution should be observed in this respect as it does not require contact alone, to infect a healthy person with the deadly virus of the fever. Breathing the same atmosphere with the infected or coming under the influence of the effluvia rising from their clothes is, in some states of the healthy body, perfectly sufficient for effecting a lodgement of the disease in the human frame. On Monday evening last the report of the Finance Committee on the subject of erecting a House of Refuge for the destitute persons who have sought refuge in our City, was received by the Council. This committee report in favour of erecting immediately such a building as would shield those from the securities of winter and recommend that a sum not exceeding $5,000 should be expended for that purpose and that this sum should be put under the joint superintendence of the Board of Works and the Finance Committee so that now we have from the praiseworthy benevolence and alacrity of the Council, an assured hope that the emigrants will not be exposed to any hardships which it is in the power of the city authorities to ward off.

The reader will bear in mind that the above relates in the city of Toronto, in Western Canada, at a distance of upwards of 500 miles from the Quarantine station whose stringent regulations were intended to protect the country from contagion.

It now only remains for me to say a few words respecting the people that endured and reproduced so much tribulation.

The vast number of persons who quitted Europe to seek new homes in the western hemisphere in the year 1847, is without a precedent in history. Of the aggregate I cannot definitely speak but to be within the limits of truth, they exceeded 350,000. More than one half of these emigrants were from Ireland and to this portion was confined the devouring pestilence. It is a painful task to trace the causes that led to such fatal consequences – some of them may perhaps be hidden but many are too plainly visible. These wretched people were flying from known misery into unknown and tenfold aggravated misfortune. That famine which compelled so many to emigrate became itself a cause of the pestilence. But that the principal causes were produced by injustice and neglect, is plainly proven.

Many, as I have already stated, were sent out at the expense of their landlords. These were consequently the poorest and most abject of the whole and suffered the most. No doubt the motives of some landlords were benevolent but all they did was to pay for the emigrants' passage – this done, these gentlemen washed their hands of all accountability transferring them to the shipping agent whose object was to stow away the greatest possible number between the decks of the vessels chartered for the purpose. That unwarrantable inducements were held out to many I am aware, causing some to leave their homes who would not otherwise have done so. They were given to understand that they would be abundantly provided for during the voyage and that they were certain of finding immediate employment upon their arrival at a dollar per day.

Another serious injury was done to many families who had previously experienced the blessings of temperance from being, upon their arrival at the different ports where they were to embark, obliged to lodge in public houses of the worst description whose proprietors, knowing that they possessed a little stock of money, seduced them to violate their 'pledge' under the specious pretext that they were no longer bound by its obligations and that whiskey was the very best preventive of seasickness.

After a detention, often of many days, the vessel at length ready for sea, numbers were shipped that were quite unfit for a long voyage. True they were inspected and so were the ships but from the limited number of officers appointed for the purpose, many oversights occurred. In Liverpool, for instance, if I am rightly informed, there was staff of but five or six men to inspect the mass of emigrants and survey the ships in which there sailed from that port 107,474.

An additional heavy infliction was their sufferings on ship-board from famine – the legal allowance for an adult being one pound of food in twenty-four hours. But perhaps the most cruel wrong was in allowing crowds of already in-

89

fected beings to be huddled up together in the confined holds, there to propagate the distemper which there was no physician to stay. The sufferings consequent upon such treatment I have endeavoured to portray in the previous narrative which – alas! – is but a feeble picture of the unmitigated trials endured by these most unhappy beings. Nor were their sufferings ended with the voyage. Oh, no! – far from it. Would that I could represent the afflictions I witnessed at Grosse Isle! I would not be supposed to think that the medical officers situated there did not exercise the greatest humanity in administering their disagreeable duties which consisted not in relieving the distress of the emigrants but in protecting their country from contamination. Still, it was most afflicting that after combating the dangers of the sea, enduring famine, drought and sickness, the wretched survivors should still have to lie as uncared for as when in the centre of the Atlantic Ocean.

The inefficacy of the quarantine system is so apparent that it is needless to particularise its defects, neither need I repeat the details of the grievous aggravations of their trials heaped by it upon the already tortured emigrants. My heart bleeds when I think of the agony of the poor families – who, as yet undivided, had patiently borne their trials, ministering to each other's wants – when torn from each other. Painful as it was to behold the bodies of those who died at sea committed to the deep, yet the separation of families was fraught with much greater misery. And as if to reach the climax of endurance, the relatives and friends of those landed upon the island were at once carried away from them to a distance of 200 miles. On their way to Montreal many died on board the steamers. There, those who sickened in their progress were received into the hospital and the survivors of this second sifting were sent on to Kingston, 180 miles further, from thence to Toronto and so on, every city and town being anxious to be rid of them. Nor were there wanting, villains who preyed upon these stricken people. The *Montreal Herald* of 13 October thus writes:

> The rapid closing of the season of course diminishes the number of arrivals of emigrants and thus the hospitals and asylums are less crowded than they have been at an earlier period of the year. The statements are, however, still extremely distressing. An assertion has been made in the Common Council and is generally believed to be true that considerable sums have been brought here by some of these people and consigned by them in their last moments, to persons who have in many instances appropriated the money to their own use. An Alderman named Tully who is known to have the means of information, calculates the average of the sums brought to Canada by emigrants at £10 each, we suppose heads of families.

In a tour which I made through Upper Canada I met in every quarter some of my poor wandering fellow-countrypeople. Travelling from Prescott to Bytown by stage, I saw a poor woman with an infant in her arms and a child pulling at her skirt and crying as they went along. The driver compassionately took them up and the wayfarer wept her thanks. She had lost her husband upon the voyage and was going to Bytown to her brother who came out the previous year and, having made some money by lumbering in the woods, remitted to her the means of joining him. She told her sad tale most plaintively and the passengers all sympathised with her. The road being of that description called 'corduroy' and the machine very crazy, the latter broke down within 5 miles of our destination and as she was unable to carry her two children, the poor creature was obliged to remain upon the road all the night. She came into Bytown the following morning and I had the satisfaction to learn that she found her brother.

A large proportion of the emigrants who arrived in Canada, crossed the frontiers in order to settle in the United States, so that they were to be seen in the most remote places. At St Catherine's upon the Welland Canal, 600 miles from Quebec, I saw a family who were on their way to the western part of the state of New York. One of them was taken ill and they were obliged to remain by the wayside

91

with nothing but a few boards to protect them from the weather. There is no means of learning how many of the survivors of so many ordeals were cut off by the inclemency of a Canadian winter so that the grand total of the human sacrifice will never be known but by 'Him who knoweth all things'.

As I cannot so well convey my sentiments in my own language I will conclude with the following quotation from England's most popular writer, and would that his suggestions uttered five years before the commencement of the tragic drama had been attended to in time: if they had, much evil had been spared humanity.

The whole system of shipping and conveying these unfortunate persons is one that stands in need of thorough revision. If any class deserve to be protected and assisted by the government, it is that class who are banished from their native land in search of the bare means of subsistence. All that could be done for those poor people by the great compassion and humanity of the captain and officers, was done but they require much more. The law is bound, at least upon the English side, to see that too many of them are not put on board one ship and that their accommodations are decent, not demoralising and profligate. It is bound too, in common humanity to declare that no man shall be taken on board without his stock of provisions being previously inspected by some proper officer and pronounced moderately sufficient for his support upon the voyage. It is bound to provide or to require that there be provided a medical attendant; whereas in these ships there are none, though sickness of adults and deaths of children on the passage are matters of the very commonest occurrence. Above all, it is the duty of any government, be it monarchy or republic, to interpose and put an end to that system by which a firm of traders in emigrants purchase of the owners the whole 'tween-decks of a ship and send on board as many wretched people as they can get hold of on any terms they can get, without the smallest reference to the conveniences of the steerage, the number of berths, the slightest separation of sexes, or any thing but their own immediate profit. Nor is this the worst of the vicious system, for certain crimping agents of these houses, who have a percentage of all the passengers they inveigle, are constantly travelling about those districts where poverty and discontent are rife and tempting the credulous into more misery, by holding out monstrous inducements to emigration which never can be realised.

Dickens, American Ketes

Epilogue

Men judge by the complexion of the sky,
The state and inclination of the day:
So may you by my dull and heavy eye,
My tongue hath but a heavier tale to say.
I play the torturer by small and small
To lengthen out the worst that may be spoken.
Shakespeare

Emigration has for a long time been considered by British political economists the most effective means of alleviating the grievous ills under which the Irish peasantry labour. It is not our province to enquire into its expediency; but viewing the subject with the single eye of common sense it is difficult to see the necessity of expatriating the superfluous population of a country wherein hundreds of thousands of acres of land susceptible of the highest culture, lie waste, whose mines teeming with wealth remain unworked and which is bordered by more than 2,000 miles of sea coast whose banks swarm with ling, cod, mackerel, etc, while salt-fish is largely imported from Scotland.

Many years previous to legislators taking up the matter, emigration from Ireland existed – and that of a class of persons which could be badly spared from the already impoverished island, consisting as it did of small but substantial farmers who, perceiving but a gloomy prospect before them, sold off their land and, turning their capital into cash, availed themselves of the opportunities that existed to find comfort and independence by settling in America.

The majority of these adventurers being successful in their undertakings, they induced their relatives and friends to follow them and thus a strong tide of emigrants whose number gradually increased each season, set toward the West.

This progressive and natural system of emigration, however, gave place within the last few years to a violent rush of famished, reckless human beings, flying from their native land to seek food in a distant and unknown country.

The cause of this sudden change is easily ascertained. Everyone is familiar with the wretched lot of the Irish peasantry: obliged to work for a miserable pittance, their chief reliance was upon the crop of potatoes grown by each family in the little patch of ground attached to their hut – a poor dependence indeed, not only as regards the inferiority of the potato as the sole diet of a people, but from the great uncertainty always attending its propagation. The consequences of even a partial failure – an event of common occurrence – were, therefore, of the most serious nature.

In the year 1822, the deficiency was so general that the price quadrupled and the peasantry of the south and west were reduced to actual starvation. To alleviate the distress, a committee was formed in London and subcommittees throughout England, and such was the benevolence of individuals that large funds were in a short time at their disposal. By the end of the year, subscriptions had been raised in Great Britain amounting to £350,000 to which parliament added a grant of £150,000, making altogether £500,000 – a large sum, but how inadequate to meet the wants of some three or four millions of starving people!

This serious warning it should be supposed would have opened the eyes of the country to the necessity of having something else as a resource under similar emergency, but a plentiful season lulled them into forgetfulness of what they had suffered, and apathy concerning the future.

So abundant was the produce of the seasons 1842 and 1843 that the poorest beggar refused potatoes and they were commonly used to manure the land.

However, the blight of the crop of 1845 and the total destruction of that of 1846 brought the country to the lowest ebb, and famine with its attendant, disease, stalked through the land.

Charity stretched forth her hand from far and near,

America giving liberally of her abundance. But all that could be done fell far short of the wants of the dying sufferers. The government stepped forward and advanced funds for the establishment of public works; this was attended with much advantage and mitigated a great deal of distress but unfortunately all the money had to be returned in the shape of onerous taxation upon the landowners.

The gentry became seriously alarmed and some of them, perceiving that the evil was likely to increase year after year, took into their consideration what would be the surest method of terminating it.

At length it was discovered that the best plan would be to get completely rid of those who were so heavy a burden upon them by shipping them to America; at the same time publishing to the world as an act of brotherly love and kindness, a deed of crafty, calculating selfishness: for the expense of transporting each individual was less than the cost of one year's support in a workhouse.

It required but little argument to induce the prostrated people to accede to their landlords' proposal by quitting their poverty-stricken country for 'a land flowing with milk and honey' – poor creatures, they thought that any change would be for the better. They had nothing to risk, everything to gain. 'Ah! Sir,' said a fellow passenger to me after bewailing the folly that tempted him to plunge his family into aggravated misfortune, 'we thought we couldn't be worse off than we war but now to our sorrow we know the differ for sure supposin' we were dyin' of starvation or if sickness overtuk us, we had a chance of a doctor and if he could do no good for our bodies sure the priest could for our souls and then we'd be buried along wid our own people, in the ould churchyard, with the green sod over us, instead of dying like rotten sheep thrown into a pit, and the minit the breath is out of our bodies flung into the sea to be eaten up by them horrid sharks.'

It cannot excite the least surprise that these wretched

beings should carry with them the seeds of that plague from which they were flying and it was but natural that these seeds should rapidly germinate in the hot-bed holds of ships crammed almost to suffocation with their distempered bodies. In short, nothing was wanted to encourage the speedy development of the direst disease and misery but – alas! – everything that could check their spread was absent.

My heart sickens when I think upon the fatal scenes of the awfully tragic drama enacted upon the wide stage of the Atlantic Ocean in the floating lazar houses that were wafted upon its bosom during the never-to-be-forgotten year 1847.

Without a precedent in history, may God grant that this account of it may descend to posterity without a parallel.

Laws for the regulation of passenger ships were in existence but, whether on account of difficulty arising from the vast augmentation of number or some other cause, they (if at all put in force) proved quite ineffectual.

What a different picture was presented by the Germans who migrated in large bodies who – although the transmission of human beings from Fatherland must always be attended by more or less pain and trouble – underwent none of those heartrending trials reserved exclusively for the Irish emigrant.

Never did so many souls tempt all the dangers of the deep to seek asylum in an adopted country and, could we draw a veil over the sad story of the ship pestilence,

> ... this migration of masses, numbering of late years more than 100,000 annually, now to nearly 300,000 annually, not in the warlike spirit of the Goths and Vandals who over-ran the Roman Empire and destroyed the monuments of art and evidences of civilization but in the spirit of peace, anxious to provide for themselves and their children the necessaries of life and apparently ordained by Providence to relieve the countries of the old world and to serve great purposes of good to mankind, is one of the most interesting spectacles the world ever saw.[1]

---

1 J. Chickering, *Immigration into the United States*, Boston, 1848

The reader must not expect to find anything more in these pages than a faithful detail of the occurrences on board an emigrant vessel. The author has no desire to exaggerate, were it possible to do so. And he who wishes to arrive at any conclusion as to the amount of suffering – he must calculate, from the affliction that I have faintly portrayed upon a small scale what must have been the unutterable 'weight of woe' in ships whose holds contained five or six hundred tainted, famished, dying mortals.

The following extract from the London *Times* newspaper presents a faithful and graphic review of the dire tragedy:

The great Irish famine and pestilence will have a place in that melancholy series of similar calamities to which historians and poets have contributed so many harrowing details and touching expressions. Did Ireland possess a writer endued with the laborious truth of Thucydides, the graceful felicity of Virgil, or the happy invention of De Foe, the events of this miserable year might be quoted by the scholar for ages to come, together with the sufferings of the pent-up multitudes of Athens, the distempered plains of northern Italy, or the hideous ravages of our own great plague. But time is ever improving on the past. There is one horrible feature of the recent, not to say present, visitation, which is entirely new. The fact of more than a hundred thousand souls flying from the very midst of a calamity across a great ocean to a new world, crowding into insufficient vessels, scrambling for a footing on a deck, or a berth in a hold, committing themselves to these worse than prisons while their frames were wasted with ill fare and their blood infected with disease, fighting for months of unutterable wretchedness against the elements without and pestilence within, giving almost hourly victims to the deep, landing at length on shores already terrified and diseased, consigned to encampments of the dying and the dead, spreading death wherever they roam and having no other prospect before them than a long continuance of these horrors in a still farther flight across forests and lakes under a Canadian sun and a Canadian frost – all these are circumstances beyond the experience of the Greek historian or Latin poet and such as an Irish pestilence alone could produce.

By the end of the season there is little doubt that the emigration into Canada alone will have amounted to 100,000, nearly all from Ireland. We know the condition in which these poor creatures embarked on their perilous adventure. They were only flying from one form of death. On the authority of the Montreal Board of Health we are enabled to say that they were allowed to ship in numbers two or three times greater than the same vessels would have presumed to carry to any

United States port.

The worse horrors of that slave-trade which it is the boast or the ambition of this empire to suppress at any cost, have been re-enacted in the flight of Irish subjects from their native shores. In only ten of the vessels that arrived at Montreal in July – four from Cork and six from Liverpool – out of 4,427 passengers, 804 had died on the passage and 847 were sick on their arrival; that is 847 were visibly diseased for the result proves that a far larger number had in them the seeds of disease. The *Larch* says the Board of Health, on 12 August – reported this morning from Sligo – sailed with 440 passengers of whom 108 died on the passage and 150 were sick.

The *Virginius* sailed with 596; 158 died on the passage, 186 were sick and the remainder landed feeble and tottering; the captain, mates and crew were all sick.

The Blackhole of Calcutta was a mercy compared to the holds of these vessels. Yet simultaneously, as if in reproof of those on whom the blame of all this wretchedness must fall, foreigners – Germans from Hamburg and Bremen – are daily arriving, healthy, robust and cheerful.

This vast unmanageable tide of population thus thrown upon Montreal, like the fugitives from some bloody defeat or devastated country, has been greatly augmented by the prudent and we must add, most necessary precautions adopted in time by the United States, where most stringent sanitary regulations, enforced by severe penalties, have been adopted to save the ports of the Union from those very horrors which a paternal government has suffered to fall upon Montreal. Many of these pest ships have been obliged to alter their destination even while at sea, for the St Lawrence.

At Montreal a large proportion of these outcasts have lingered from sheer inability to proceed. The inhabitants of course have been infected.

A still more horrible sequel is to come. The survivors have to wander forth and find homes. Who can say how many will perish on the way or the masses of houseless, famished and half-naked wretches that will be strewed on the inhospitable snow when a Canadian winter sets in?

Of these awful occurrences some account must be given. Historians and politicians will some day sift and weigh the conflicting narratives and documents of this lamentable year and pronounce with or without affectation, how much is due to the inclemency of heaven and how much to the cruelty, heartlessness or improvidence of man. The boasted institutions and spirit of the empire are on trial. They are weighed in the balance.

Famine and pestilence are at the gates and the conscience-stricken nation will almost fear to see the 'writing on the wall'.

We are forced to confess that, whether it be the fault of our laws or our men, this new act in the terrible drama has not been met as humanity and common sense would enjoin. The result was quite within the scope of calculation and even of care.

Miscalculation and want of care, are terms far too mild to apply to such wanton negligence as resulted in the immediate sacrifice of upwards of 25,000 souls, four-fifths of whom fell upon their way to Canada. From the report issued at the end of the season, it appears that, of the 98,105 (of whom 60,00 were Irish) that were shipped for Quebec,

There died at sea,	5,293
At Grosse Isle and Quebec,	8,072
In and above Montreal,	7,000
Making	20,365

besides those who afterwards perished, whose number can never be ascertained. Allowing an average of 300 persons to each, 200 vessels were employed in the transmission to Canada of Irish emigrants alone, and each of these vessels lost one-third of her living cargo ere she again set sail upon her return to Europe.

If we suppose those 60,000 persons to be an army on their way to invade some hostile power, how serious would appear the loss of one-third of their number before a battle was fought? Yet the 40,000 who landed upon the Canadian shores had to fight many a deadly battle before they could find peace or rest. Or, in order to make the matter sensible to those who know the value of money better than of human life, let us multiply 20,000 by 5, the cost in pounds sterling of the passage of each individual and we perceive a loss of £100,000 or $500,000.

However, it may be thought that the immolation of so many wretched starvelings was rather a benefit than a loss to the world. It may be so. Yet, untutored, degraded, famished and plague-stricken, as they were I assert that there was more true heroism, more faith, more forgiveness to their enemies and submission to the Divine Will exemplified in these victims, than could be found in ten times the number of their oppressors.

APPENDIX I

IRISH FEAR PARK WILL IGNORE THEIR HISTORY
Irish Panel urged to protect sanctity of site
(Containing Norita Fleming's Speech)[1]

Environment Canada has raised the ire of the Irish with its plans to turn Grosse Île into a national park.

'The development concept … is unacceptable,' Pádraig O'Laighin, a director of the St Patrick's Society of Montreal, told a public hearing last night.

O'Laighin echoed the sentiments of 11 Irish-group leaders who presented their concerns to a four-member panel for Environment Canada's parks service.

The federal government intends to develop the former quarantine station of Grosse Île, about 45 kilometres downstream from Quebec City, into a historic theme park – Canada: Land of Welcome and Hope.

But the Irish community is upset because Grosse Île holds the graves of several thousand immigrants who died there of typhoid fever in 1847 after they fled the Great Famine in Ireland.

'Outside of Ireland, Grosse Île is recognised by us as the most important and evocative Great Famine site on earth,' said Don Mullan, who travelled from Dublin on Tuesday to address the public hearing at the downtown Guy Favreau Conference Centre yesterday.

Mullan, director of Action From Ireland's Great Famine Project, said he made the trip across the Atlantic 'to ensure that the sanctity of Grosse Île, as a place of profound Irish significance, is protected and preserved.'

Representatives of most of the groups took issue with a

---

1 Reprinted with permission from the *Gazette*, Thursday, 21 May 1992

portion of the federal government's published development plan for the island that suggests 'there should not be too much emphasis on the tragic history of Grosse Île'.

'Under no circumstances can we condone the denial or concealment of truth, especially historic truth,' argued Pat O'Shea, president of the Tara Golf Association Inc.

'No more than the Jewish people would want to relegate to oblivion the tragedy of Treblinka would the Irish people want to forget the tragedy and historic significance of Grosse Île,' O'Shea said.

'That historic island is our Treblinka, for it enshrouds in mass graves the mortal remains of more than 12,000 native Irish men, women and children.'

Earlier yesterday, the committee heard five submissions from private individuals.

The most emotional came from Norita Fleming of Toronto, who urged the committee to make sure that Grosse Île's grim role in the history of Canada's Irish population be fully explained in any attempt to transform the site into a historic park.

Fleming, a native of Ireland, cited contemporary news reports, published in the *Gazette* in 1847, which recalled scenes of Irish immigrants dying from typhus en route to Grosse Île on 'coffin ships' or perishing in 'fever sheds' on Grosse Île, in Montreal or Quebec City.

'Today, we owe our people the protection, the preservation and acknowledgement of their burial ground, their hallowed graveyards,' she said.

'An apology and an acknowledgement of this happening has to be established.

'The historic site of Grosse Île has to be acknowledged as the graveyard of the Irish famine victims – dedicated to their courage and their suffering, sacred to their memory.'

Panel chairman Laurent Tremblay reminded the more than 100 people who appeared at yesterday's hearings that the parks service will begin studying all the recommendations and suggestions at the end of September.

NORITA FLEMING'S SPEECH TO THE MONTREAL PANEL

A Chara,[2]

I am writing this letter in response to some misrepresentation of the historical record of Irish immigration to Canada, that you put forward in your Development Concept, March 1992:

> Vast numbers of Irish have left their country since the 1820s to escape overpopulation, repeated food shortages and the re-allocation of land by landlords and, from 1845, the great potato famine [p.9].

This claim that impersonal economic forces, not British colonialism, lay behind the suffering and death is untrue. Also the proposal to conceal the real history of Grosse Île:

> It is also felt that there should not be too much emphasis on the tragic aspects of the history of Grosse Île. On the contrary, the painful events of 1832 and 1847, which have been over-emphasised in the past, need to be put back into perspective without robbing them of their importance [p.62].

I am writing this letter to you to go on record at our public hearings in Montreal, 20 May 1992, stating that the immigrants who fled Ireland between 1832 and 1860 ... and who died in their thousands in the coffin ships and fever sheds in Canada, were driven from their homes by the English government, whose policy was to clear the land. Further, that the holocaust of suffering inflicted on the Irish people not go unrecorded.

In 1847 when the most devastating of all the potato blight and famine ensued, Canada was still serving under the Union Jack. The greatest tragedy of the 1847 famine was

---

2 'A Chara' is the Irish for 'Dear Friend'

that it never should have happened. The contradiction of that famine was that in one of the richest agricultural lands in the world, people were dying of starvation. The food that was being produced was taken for payment of rent and shipped out of the country under armed guard. The only food left for the poor tenant farmer was the potato and perhaps some cabbage and turnips. With the failure of the potato, mass starvation erupted. People were dying so fast that their surviving relatives were unable to bury them. They were starving from an artificially created famine, the result of the force of a relentless universal power. This was the contrived plan of a group of landlords – to starve the people to death and rid the Irish of the land since they proved an encumbrance to them. This was an immigration of mass expulsion, not of free choice.

The ships contracted to aid and abet the greedy landlords were usually logging vessels on their return voyage – having unloaded their cargo of wood, they reloaded with a cargo of humanity; in the hole of the ships that would perpetuate human suffering, degradation, disease and death in its thousands. There are no accurate accounts of the numbers buried at sea but it is commonly accepted that from Ireland to Grosse Île, in the ocean graveyard, bodies could form a continuous chain of burial crosses. During the ocean voyage further injustices were inflicted on the people with bad water and near non-existent food provisions, that added to the human misery.

The Irish people between 1832 and 1860 were a people driven from their homeland by persecution and deprivation of human rights. The knowledge of the shocking mistreatment of the immigrants during the voyage and their subsequent arrival at Grosse Île, broken in health with thousands suffering from typhus, was information deliberately repressed. The policy of the government then, according to a complaint to the *Kingston Chronicle*, 17 June 1848, was to keep the news of what was happening at Grosse Île from leaking out.

However, articles were making headlines elsewhere. An article in the *Gazette*, Montreal, 5 September 1847, reads as follows, referring to the fever sheds at Point St Charles:

> In the hastily erected emergency sheds the people were dying by the score, in the stench and heat, desperately neglected. When there were enough attendants they were hastily tossed into shallow pits nearby where they succumbed to the fever. In all the history of Montreal there is no story more poignant. There were hundreds of orphaned children. Many of the little ones had to be pulled from the arms of parents who had suddenly died. Older ones were wandering around frantically looking for parents who were already buried in the pits. The scene in the children's shed was beyond description.

It has been proffered that some of the evidence and many of the records of that period were destroyed by fire. In 1909, in a book by Jordan, *The Grosse Île Tragedy*, the silence was finally broken after 50 years. The island was further held out of reach by making it into a quarantine for cattle, preventing it from becoming a focus. Today we owe our people the preservation and acknowledgement of their burial ground, their Hallowed Graveyard. The Irish people who died through forced starvation, forced separation and immigration from their lands were obliged to travel on vessels that were for many to become their coffins. On their subsequent arrival at Grosse Île they were destined to die in their thousands, in the poorly erected fever sheds on that tragic Île and in Quebec, Montreal, Kingston, Toronto and in other places. Those who were criminally responsible for this human holocaust teach us that there is no limit to human depravity when man is motivated by greed, wealth, power and prestige. The perpetuators and collaborators of these events caused the Irish people untold grief and suffering. They paid for it in the thousands with their lives. An apology and an acknowledgement of this happening has to be established. This historic site at Grosse Île has to be acknowledged as the island graveyard of the Irish famine victims, dedicated to their courage and sufferings, sacred to their memory. By this acknowledgement, the debt owed to them can be set right by remembering.

Norita Fleming
Ontario

c.c. Hon. Brian Mulroney
c.c. Hon. Sean Charest
c.c. Hon. Teresa Pamelo

APPENDIX II

THE CLERGY AND THE PLAGUE[1]

'Greater love than this no man hath ...'

On the pedestal of a monument in City Hall Square Quebec, there is an impressive bronze plaque erected to the memory of Elzear Alexandre Tachereau, later known as Cardinal Tachereau. The plaque shows a scene at Grosse Île. A priest and some nuns are attending the sick and dying. (Representing nuns at Grosse Île seems to be an error. They are not mentioned in any of the records.) In the background, out in the harbour, one of the emigrant sailing vessels is shown. Tachereau was a young priest, newly ordained, when he volunteered for service at the Grosse Île quarantine station during the disastrous summer months of 1847. The plaque was intended as a tribute, not only to young Fr Tachereau, but to all the clergy who offered their services during that fateful period.

When Tachereau and his companion, Edward John Horan, later first secretary of Laval University and then Bishop of Kingston, left for Grosse Île they were fully aware of the risk they were taking. There would be little hope of escaping the contagion. Though hunger and poor sanitation contributed more than anything else to the progress of the disease it spared no class, neither rich nor poor, neither the well-fed nor the hungry. It often struck with lightning swiftness. In Ireland, for example, whole families were known to have perished overnight. Their shielings had to be levelled over their bodies to bury them. On Grosse Île thousands of the emigrants were easy victims of its ravages, weakened and starved as they were after the ocean voyage. Into this world of contagion came clergymen, both Catholic and Anglican,

---

1 Taken from *The Voyage of the Naparima*

who joined with the doctors and other attendants in ministering to the needs of the mass of suffering humanity they found there.

No missionary to a foreign land ever faced the hardships that these men endured during the summer of Black '47. The severest of all their trials was to be exposed day and night to the indescribable misery of the patients in their fever sheds. For them the sense of loneliness and abandonment, from loss of relatives and other friends, was no less painful than the ravages of fever, hunger and dysentery. The foul odours and the filthy conditions in general in the sheds made the atmosphere stifling even when there was a breeze from the river.

Of Irish and French Canadian priests and Anglican clergymen, over 40 served on Grosse Île. It is not known exactly how many died but a number did succumb to the fever. Most of them contracted it and recovered. Tachereau and Horan were only a short time exercising their ministry when they became afflicted. After a brief convalescence in Quebec they insisted on returning and left only when there were no more patients to care for.

As mentioned elsewhere, the clergy were on call so much that they literally slept with their boots on. The nights were often busier than the days. What little rest they got was punctuated with the nightmarish sounds of the carts hauling more bodies to the trenches and the mournful sounds from the sheds.

An enviable spirit of co-operation and mutual support existed among this group of clergy, representing two languages and two denominations. The French priests usually called on an Irish confrère when a language problem came up, though, in general, through the use of Latin and what English they knew, they were able to get along. Anglicans and Catholics co-operated in getting the patients their own clergy to serve their spiritual needs. No lines were drawn when there was question of offering a little help in making the patients more comfortable. At times such simple attentions as offering a noggin of water or speaking a word of comfort was enough to revive the sagging spirit of a disconsolate sufferer. There was no limit to the kind of service the clergy offered.

The records show that seventeen Protestant clergy volunteered to serve on Grosse Île. This signifies extraordinary generosity on their part since only about 10 per cent of the patients were Protestant, mostly Anglican. Among the seventeen, seven contracted the fever and two, Reverend Richard Anderson and Reverend Charles Morris, died.

The leader of the Anglican group was the distinguished George Jehosophat Mountain, later known as Bishop Mountain. Like the other clergymen he did not hesitate to render every kind of service to the fever victims. Though obliged to leave the island twice, he returned to complete his ministry. In his memoirs, edited by his son Armine, the following comment appears:

> The general thankfulness of the patients on receiving ministrations, the examples of faith, resignation and gratitude are most pleasing to behold. There is practically no murmuring or bewailing of conditions.

He observed, in another part of his memoirs, that, in spite of the revolting conditions of the fever sheds, he experienced much consolation in serving the sick and dying. In a similar vein, Fr McGauran, one of the Irish priests, made the following observations:

> I can assure you that never in my life have I felt such consolation. The blessings of the sick and dying soothe all my own pains.

And Fr Tachereau has been quoted as saying:

> My only regret is for not having come here (to Grosse Île) sooner and my only worry now is that I may have to leave the island to allow other priests a chance to have their turn.

Many among the clergy who did not serve on the island directed their zeal towards caring for orphans. One of the Irish emigrants recalled, many years after that fateful summer, a touching incident that took place in the Basilica in Quebec. It was during Sunday Mass. At the time for the sermon the priest led two children with him into the pulpit. It was disclosed later on that day, that the priest was Monsignor Baillargeon, acting Bishop of Quebec. And the children were two little Irish orphans. The parishioners were told that there were hundreds of children like these two, left homeless, after losing parents and relatives on the ocean and at the Quarantine station. Monsignor Baillargeon appealed to them to take the children into their homes.

Several of the clergy and nuns lost their lives. They practically all suffered grave inconveniences from fatigue and mental anguish over the sufferings they witnessed and from attacks of the fever. But like their counterparts at Grosse Île they found ample reward in the grateful expressions of those they ministered to and above all in the conviction that they were privileged in being called to co-operate in a mission of mercy.

The Annals of the Hôtel Dieu mention eight priests, including the Vicar-General himself, M.H. Hudon, who lost their lives tending the fever victims. Five of these priests were Sulpicians. Fr McInerney, curate of Lachine, died at Montreal. The Reverend Patrick Colgan died at St Andrews. Bishop Bourger himself was stricken down with the fever. It was said that the bishop and his vicar-general alternated in the night watches over the sick and dying. Fr Charbonnel fortunately recovered. An editorial in *The Pilot* of 10 July 1847, pays the following tribute:

> There never surely was any Church which in the times of the most fiery persecution proved, at the sacrifice of comfort and life, its devotion to religion, more signally than does now the Roman Catholic clergy of Montreal.

It was Divine protection surely that all did not die.

Among those who lost their lives as a result of being attacked by the fever at Pointe St Charles was one of Montreal's most distinguished citizens, Mayor John Easton Mills. His visits to the fever sheds went far beyond the requirements of official surveillance. He took on the duties of a voluntary nurse. He was in constant attendance among the sick and dying and abandoned. *The Courier*, Montreal, claimed that:

> He was at the sheds every day, sometimes for hours on end and was often seen at the bedside of a dying emigrant administering the greatest of all possible relief – human comfort.

Mayor Mills died from the fever in his fifty-first year. He was a martyr, having risked his life to serve his neighbour.

Not to be outdone by his priests, the Chief Pastor, Bishop Power, helped out in the fever sheds, trying to bring physical as well as spiritual comfort to as many patients as he could reach. Late one September night, around midnight, a call came to his residence requesting the last Sacraments for a woman who was dying of the fever. Bishop Power answered the call and had the consolation of anointing the poor woman just before she died. Next day he developed symptoms of the dread disease and in a few days it developed into its most virulent form. He died on 1 October and, as the cathedral was still unfinished, the funeral service was held at St Paul's. Fr Kelly described the funeral procession in the following words:

> The cortège proceeded by way of Power, King and Church streets and, as a tribute of respect, the stores along the line of march were closed. Silent thousands, non-Catholics as well as Catholics, were on the sidewalks to pay their tribute to the memory of a man whom they revered as a saint, a scholar, a friend and an outstanding citizen of their community.

APPENDIX III

ON THE ISLAND: THE HORRORS OF GROSSE ISLE[1]

Published in *The Grosse Île Tragedy* by: J. Jordan in 1909

> Immediately a place
> Before his eyes appeared, sad, noisome, dark
> A lazar-house it seem'd; wherein were laid
> Numbers of all diseased; all maladies of
> Ghastly spasm or racking torture, qualms
> Of heart-sick agony, all feverous kinds,
> Marasmus and wide-wasting pestilence.
> Dire was the tossing, deep the groans: Despair
> Tended the sick, busiest from couch to couch;
> And over them triumphant Death his dart
> Shook, but delay'd to strike, though oft invok'd
> With vows, as their chief good, and final hope.
> Sight so deform what heart of rock could long
> Dry-eyed behold?
>
> *Milton*

The Canadian authorities were hardly less remiss than the British in preparations to meet the terrible emergency before them; although they had equally received ample warning of it. In 1846, Dr Douglas, the medical superintendent at Grosse Isle, had repeatedly urged them to get ready for what was coming. The British, Irish, American and Canadian newspapers had almost daily reported and commented on the alarming progress which the famine and pestilence were making in Ireland, so that they could not plead ignorance of the ominous outlook or of the fact that the emigration from the Green Isle to Canada in 1847 would

---

1 Reprinted with permission of the *Chronicle Telegraph*

be on a very large scale. Early in that year Mr Robert Christie, the historian, then a leading member of the Provincial Parliament, wrote to the Provincial Secretary, Hon. Dominick Daly, complaining of the Government's inexcusable failure to take proper and necessary precautions and pointing out the great danger to which the country would be exposed, together with the measures to be adopted to avert it. Reverend Fr Moylan, the Catholic missionary at Grosse Isle in those days, also gave timely forewarning to the Government with respect to the gravity of the situation and it was upon his urgent recommendation that, later when the crisis was on, the available police force to keep order on the island was increased by 50 men of the 93rd Regiment, under Lt Studdard, sent down from Quebec.

But all the signs and the warnings of the coming storm were virtually unheeded until it was practically too late. The only additions made to the Quarantine establishment were through the purchase of 50 bedsteads, double the quantity of straw used in former years and the erection of a new shed or building to serve as a hospital and to contain 60 more beds. In this way, provision, including the old hospitals and sheds dating from 1832, was made for only 200 sick, the average of former years never having attained half that number requiring admission at one time. How utterly inadequate this was, the alarming sequel soon showed.

But, while there was little or no excuse for the failure of the British authorities to have risen equal to the great emergency, there was certainly a good deal for that of their Canadian colleagues. At that time the British North American provinces were comparatively new and poor, carrying on a struggling existence and possessing little means or few resources that were then available. Their political and social organisation was yet in a more or less primitive and chaotic state, and as already seen, they were also divided among themselves by conflicting opinions as to the gravity of the danger and the steps to be taken to avert or meet it. However, they were very soon brought face to face with it in all its hideousness and scarcely a month had elapsed after the opening of navigation in 1847, when a session of the Provincial Parliament was hurriedly called and held in Montreal, a select committee was appointed to enquire into the situation, and a commission was also appointed consisting of Drs Painchaud, of Quebec and McDonnell and Campbell, of Montreal, to investigate the character and amount of sickness prevailing among the emigrants at Grosse Isle and the best mode to be adopted to arrest the disease and prevent its dissemination, with full powers to make all such changes on the island as they thought proper.

The commissioners reported. Of the sick in the hospitals, sheds and tents, they said:

> We found these unfortunate people in the most deplorable condition for want of necessary nurses and hospital attendants; their friends who had partially recovered being in too many instances unable and in most, unwilling, to render them any assistance, common sympathies being apparently annihilated by the mental and bodily depression produced by famine and disease. At our inspection of many of the vessels, we witnessed some appalling instances of what we have now stated – corpses lying in the same beds with the sick and the dying, the healthy not taking the trouble to remove them.

Immediate steps were taken by the commissioners for affording temporary shelter on the island, by means of spars and sails borrowed from the ships and the putting up of shanties for the accommodation of the healthy.

What pen can fittingly describe the horrors of that shocking summer at Grosse Isle? All the eye-witnesses, all the writers on the subject, agree in saying that they have never been surpassed in pathos, as well as in hideousness and ghastliness. In a few months one of the most beautiful spots on the St Lawrence was converted into a great lazar and charnel-house to be forever sanctified by the saddest memories of an unhappy race.

In speaking of the fever sheds, Mr De Vere says:

113

They were very miserable, so slightly built as to exclude neither the heat nor the cold. No sufficient care was taken to remove the sick from the sound or to disinfect and clean the beddings. The very straw upon which they had lain was often allowed to become a bed for their successors and I have known many poor families prefer to burrow under heaps of loose stones, near the shore, rather than accept the shelter of the infected sheds.

Captain, afterwards Admiral Boxer, of Crimean fame, stated that there was nothing more terrible than the sheds. Most of the patients were attacked with dysentery and the smell was dreadful, as there was no ventilation.

Frs Moylan and O'Reilly saw the emigrants in the sheds lying on the bare boards and ground for whole nights and days without either bed or bedding. Two, and sometimes three, were in a berth. No distinction was made as to sex, age or nature of illness. Food was insufficient and the bread not baked. Patients were supplied three times a day with tea, gruel or broth. How any of them ever recovered is a wonder. Fr O'Reilly visited two ships, the *Avon* and the *Triton*. The former lost 136 passengers on the voyage and the latter 93. All these were thrown overboard and buried in the Atlantic. He administered the last rites to over 200 sick on board these ships. Fr Moylan's description of the condition of the holds of these vessels is simply most revolting and horrible.

As for the dead, who were not buried at sea, it has been already seen how they were taken from the pest ships and corded like firewood on the beach to await burial. In many instances the corpses were carried out of the foul smelling holds or they were dragged with boat-hooks out of them by sailors and others who had to be paid a sovereign for each.

A word more as to the removal of the corpses from the vessels. They were brought from the hold, where the darkness was, as it were, rendered more visible by the miserable untrimmed oil lamp that showed light in some places sufficient to distinguish a form, but not a face. It was more by touch than by sight that the passengers knew each other.

First came the touch and then the question, who is it? Even in the bunks many a loved one asked the same question to one by his or her side, for in the darkness that reigned their eyesight was failing them.

The priest, leaving daylight and sunlight behind, as each step from deck led him down the narrow ladder into the hold of the vessels of those days, as wanting in ventilation as the Black Hole of Calcutta, had to make himself known and your poor Irish emigrant with the love and reverence he had for his clergy, who stuck to him through thick and thin, endeavoured to raise himself and warmly greet him with the little strength that remained.

Another death announced, orders were given by the captain for the removal of the body. Kind hands in many cases attended to this. In other cases, as we have seen, it was left to strangers. Up the little narrow ladder to the deck, were the corpses borne in the same condition in which they died, victims among other things of filth, uncleanliness and bed sores and with hardly any clothing on them. There was no pretence of decency or the slightest humanity shown.

On deck a rope was placed around the emaciated form of the Irish peasant, father, mother, wife and husband, sister and brother. The rope was hoisted and with their heads and naked limbs dangling for a moment in mid-air, with the wealth of hair of the Irish maiden, or young Irish matron, or the silvered locks of the poor old Irish grandmother floating in the breeze, they were finally lowered over the ship's side into the boats, rowed to the island and left on the rocks until such time as they were coffined. Well might His Grace the Archbishop of Quebec, in his letter to the Bishops of Ireland, say that the details he received of the scenes of horror and desolation at the island almost staggered belief and baffled description.

There was no delay in burying the dead. The spot selected for their last resting place was a lonely one at the western end of the island at about 10 acres from the landing. At first the graves were not dug a sufficient depth. The rough coffins were piled one over the other and the earth covering the upper row, in some instances, was not more than a foot deep and generally speaking about a foot and a half. The cemetery was about 6 acres in extent. Later huge trenches were dug in it about 5 or 6 feet deep and in these the bodies were laid often uncoffined. Six men were kept constantly employed at this work.

Béchard, in his history of the island, adds a new horror to the ghoulish scene. He states that an army of rats, which had come ashore from the fever ships, invaded the field of death, took possession of it and pierced it with innumerable holes to get at and gnaw the bodies buried in the shallow graves until hundreds of loads of earth had to be carted and placed upon them.

At first, says the late J. M. O'Leary, the sick were placed in the hospitals, while the seemingly healthy were sent to the sheds, but emigrants were continually arriving who were left for days and nights without a bed under them, or a cover over them, wasting and melting away under the united influence of fever and dysentery, without anyone to give them a drink during their long hours of raging thirst and terrible sufferings. For want of beds and bedding, for want of attendants, hundreds of poor creatures – after a long voyage consumed by confinement and hunger, thirst and disease – were compelled to spend the long, long nights and sultry days, lying on the hard boards without a pillow under their burning heads, without a hand to moisten their parched lips or fevered brows and what was the result? They who, by a little providential precaution and ordinary care, might have been restored to their large, helpless families and distracted relations, were hurried away in a few hours to their premature and unhonoured graves while those who should at once have provided for their salvation at any cost and sacrifice were haggling about the means. What encouragement was it for a young professional man to expose himself to almost certain death for the paltry remuneration of 17 shillings and 6 pence a day held out to those who tendered their services? What could be hoped for or expected from nurses who were willing to spend their nights and days in a fever hospital for 3 shillings a day?

In the sheds were double tiers of bunks, the upper one about 3 feet above the lower. As the planks of the former were not placed close together, the filth from the sick fell upon those in the lower tier who were too weak to move. Filth was thus allowed to accumulate and with so vast a crowd of fever cases in one place and with no ventilation, generated a miasma so virulent and concentrated that few who came within its poisonous atmosphere escaped. Clergy, doctors, hospital attendants, servants and police, fell ill one after the other and not a few of them succumbed. A number of the captains, officers and crews of the pest ships also died at Grosse Isle and some of the vessels were so decimated of these during the voyage across and so short-handed, that it is a wonder how they ever reached the island.

Oftentimes there were two and sometimes three in a bed without any distinction of age, sex or nature of illness. Corpses remained all night in the places where death occurred, even when there was a companion in the same bed, while the bodies that had been brought from the ships were piled like cordwood on the beach without any covering over them until such time as they were coffined.

In the midst of this fierce Canadian summer, thousands of sick kept pouring into Grosse Isle. Not a drop of fresh water was to be found on the island, no lime juice, no clean straw even to protect the patients from the wet ground in the tents while in the beginning of July, with the thermometer at 98° in the shade, hundreds were landed from the ships and thrown rudely by the unfeeling crews, on the burning rocks and there they remained whole nights and days without shelter of any kind.

And as if this terrible almost incredible state of affairs

117

were not sufficient, outside the hospitals no order was observed. The very police, who were appointed to maintain order, were the first to set an example of drunkenness and immorality. Is it to be wondered at then that great difficulty was experienced in retaining honest nurses or attendants who had a reputation to sustain? On those days of the week, when the opportunity of leaving the island was offered by the arrival of the steamer from Quebec, a great number of servants insisted upon their discharge but such applications were firmly refused, unless the applicants could produce a substitute. It is hardly necessary to say that many, so retained against their will, neglected their duty to the sick and sought by every means to provoke their dismissal.

Nurses were obliged to occupy a bed in the midst of the sick and had no private apartment where they could change their clothing. Their food was the same as was given to the emigrant and had to be taken in haste amid the effluvia of the sheds and in this way they were frequently infected with fever. When they fell sick they were left to themselves.

The report of these melancholy events magnified by rumour, circulated in Quebec to such an extent that none were willing to expose themselves to a fate which seemed to wait on those who had the care of the sick. What happened? The door of the common jail was thrown open and its loathsome inmates were sent to Grosse Isle to nurse the pure, helpless Irish youth.

APPENDIX IV

ÎLE OF IRISH TEARS[1]

Canada will be dedicating a new national park next year on Grosse Île in the St Lawrence river in memory of the thousands of immigrants, the Irish particularly, who died on the doorstep of their new homeland.

The tiny island sparkled an emerald green, a sharp contrast to the surrounding cold, grey waters of the St Lawrence River. As the plane circled the island which will next year become Canada's newest national park, Grosse Île portrays an image of serene beauty, a luxuriant forest covers much of the island broken only by a few clusters of buildings and the rocky shore.

A century ago and more, it was an island of sorrow, heartache and death. A tragic and largely forgotten story of Canada's early days.

Standing tall on the island's highest point is a granite Celtic cross bearing the following inscription in English, French and Gaelic:

> Sacred to the memory of thousands of Irish emigrants who, to preserve the faith, suffered hunger and exile in 1847–48 and stricken with fever ended here their sorrowful pilgrimage.
> *Erected by the Ancient Order of Hibernians in America and dedicated Feast of the Assumption, 1909.*

The 14-metre (46-foot) high cross is a grim reminder of the days when Grosse Île was Canada's first and major quarantine station. It was the first landfall in the new world and sometimes the last, for thousands fleeing the famine, poverty and persecution of their European homelands. In 105 years, from 1832 when it opened until closing in 1937, Grosse Île

---

1 Reprinted with permission from the *Toronto Star*, 2 May 1992

was the gateway into Canada for over 4 million immigrants.

In the early 1800s, sailing ships would carry timber from Canada to Britain, a major export. On the return voyage, the ships would be packed with immigrants, classified as 'paying ballast'. This was boon for landlords in Scotland, England and Ireland as they literally herded 'surplus population' and 'sources of unrest' onto the ships. What happened after that, the landlords didn't care. The newcomers were dumped on shore at Quebec City, the major port for the timber ships and Canada's main point of entry.

In 1826 an outbreak of Asiatic cholera swept across India. It spread into Europe, reaching Moscow in 1831 and the British Isles a few months later.

Fearful Canadian colonial authorities, faced with increasing waves of immigrants and no international inspection system, created a quarantine station in 1832 on Grosse Île, a small uninhabited island in the St Lawrence about 50 kilometres (30 miles) downstream from Quebec City. It is a narrow island, measuring only 2.5 km (1.5 miles) in length with an area of 185 hectares (457 acres).

The Canadians certainly had cause to worry. The previous year, 1831, saw more than 60,000 people arrive in Quebec, a city which then had barely a population of 33,000.

New regulations ordered all ships to stop at Grosse Île for inspection. A cannon was placed overlooking the river to warn ships trying to sneak past. If cholera, typhus or a contagious disease such as smallpox was found among the passengers, a blue flag was hoisted on the contaminated ship. Both sick and healthy were taken off for further tests at the island's unfinished hospitals. The island was staffed by Canadian medical personnel, soldiers and the clergy.

But the quarantine regulations weren't good enough. They leaked as badly as many of the immigrant ships. In 1832 more than 3,800 people died of cholera in Quebec, another 1,900 in Montreal. And the dreaded infection swept up the St Lawrence to Kingston, Toronto, Hamilton and Detroit.

More hospitals were built on Grosse Île to house the sick and dying, more hotels for the healthy. The cholera waves kept on hitting in 1834, in 1847 and '48 and again in 1854. At times, Grosse Île's harbour was crowded with 40 or more vessels, all flying the dreaded blue flags.

On landing, each immigrant went through showers in the disinfection building, their clothing and personal belongings were thoroughly fumigated. The sick were taken to the hospital, to lie on bunk beds in crowded dormitories. The healthy were lodged in hotels befitting their station for the 40-day quarantine period, first class for the wealthy, second class for the not-so-wealthy and third class for the poor. Only a small fence separated the areas between the sick and healthy.

Typhus, also known as 'ship fever', claimed as many or more lives than cholera. In 1847, a wave of 90,000 immigrants saw 10,000 of them dying from typhus on reaching Canada – 5,000 also died on board ships during the voyages.

From 1832 to 1860, the main flow of immigrants to Canada were from the British Isles, the majority from Ireland. The next largest were the Scots, thrown off their crofting lands during the infamous Highland Clearances when sheep replaced people in the Scottish glens. The Irish were attempting to escape the potato famine and crushing poverty which had killed hundreds of thousands. Many suffered the same fate here.

The Irish were particularly vulnerable; they were ravaged by hunger and disease even before they boarded the ramshackle ships for the long, arduous journey across the Atlantic.

The most touching and poignant sights on Grosse Île today are the four desolate cemeteries. The largest is simply a burial field with undulating mounds, adorned with a few white crosses. The sketchy records indicate there are 5,000 to 8,000 buried there in the unmarked mass graves, no one knows for sure.

Many of the Canadians helping the immigrants also died, doctors, nurses, clergy and soldiers. The surviving personnel were overworked and did not have the time to conduct proper burials or dig individual graves. Medical records sometimes list no names just the number of persons who died on a given day. Many more died on the ships in the harbour and were buried at sea. Small wonder the vessels were called 'coffin ships'.

From 1860 to the turn of the century, the rapid improvement in medicine, the switch from slow sailing ships to steam-ships and tougher international quarantine regulations slowed the spread of disease. In 1862, only 58 people died on Grosse Île, 34 from typhus. The decade from 1870 to 1880 recorded only 42 deaths from disease on Grosse Île.

The worst was over.

Grosse Île stayed as a quarantine station until 1937, doing much to halt the spread of contagious diseases, such as typhus, cholera, beriberi, smallpox and bubonic plague into Canada from other parts of the world. By then, immigrants were entering Canada at a variety of ports. Medically, the big city hospitals were better equipped to handle contagious diseases.

During the Second World War and for several years later, the island was wrapped in a mantle of secrecy when it was used by the Department of National Defence as a research station for bacteriological warfare, such as the manufacture of anthrax, an extremely virulent micro-organism. In 1956, Agriculture Canada took over the operation of the island for the quarantine and testing of animals.

HUMANE ACT

Grosse Île might have slipped away to become only a minor footnote in Canadian history, just another speck of land in the St Lawrence, but for a very selfless and humane act during the terrible years of the last century.

Thousands of children were left as orphans when their parents, mostly Irish, died on the ships or in hospital on Grosse Île. The children were taken to orphanages in Quebec City and Montreal and most were later adopted by Irish and French-Canadian families in Quebec. The church ruled the orphans were to be allowed to keep their birth names, not take the names of the adopting parents. The Grey Nuns of Quebec City kept a register of the orphans and the adopting families, a treasure for modern-day historians and genealogists.

To this day, there are families on both the north and south shores of the St Lawrence with Irish names, descendants of those who died in their quest for a new life. In the 1960s, those descendants in the Montmagny area on the south shore opposite Grosse Île started a movement to recognise the historical importance of the island.

LOTS MORE TO DO

In 1983 the Canadian government declared the island an historical site and in 1993 it will become a national historic park operated by Parks Canada. Federal officials have conducted public hearings and meetings over the past two months for input from Quebec residents on the development of the park.

'We have lots to do over the next year to make this a national park,' commented Renée Lemieux of Parks Canada, our very personable and helpful guide during a tour of the island. 'We are starting from scratch. Right now, we have very few facilities for visitors.'

At present there are a few tourist boats which make the 45-minute trip from Montmagny or the 3-hour journey from Quebec city. A private air service has 5-minute flights to the island from Montmagny landing on a postage-stamp gravel runway.

This is not Disneyland. Toilet facilities are rare on the island and other services are primitive. Only soft drinks and coffee are available in a part-time restaurant at the first-class hotel which is being partially restored. A small jitney service, similar to the small trains at the CNE, is available to take visitors on a tour of the island.

Note: French–Irish societies have been mounting a campaign against the Canadian Government plans to turn the site into a tourist attraction for gain. Bord Fáilte in English–Canada together with Irish clubs in Ottawa and Toronto are co-operating in attempting to have the site preserved as a sacred place – a monument to the thousands of Irish victims who died and are buried in heaps in the island of Grosse Île, Quebec.

The Course of Irish History

Edited by T.W. Moody and F. X. Martin

Though many specialist books on Irish history have appeared in the past fifty years, there have been few general works broadly narrating and interpreting the course of Irish history as a whole, in the light of new research. That is what this book set out to do; and it is a measure of its success that it is still in demand.

The first of its kind in its field, the book provides a rapid short survey, with geographical introduction, of the whole course of Ireland's history. Based on the series of television programmes first transmitted by Radio Telefís Éireann from January to June 1966, it is designed to be both popular and authoritative, concise but comprehensive, highly selective but balanced and fair-minded, critical but constructive and sympathetic. A distinctive feature is its wealth of illustrations.

The present edition is a revised and enlarged version of the original book. A new chapter has been added, bringing the narrative to the end of 1982, and the illustrations have been correspondingly augmented. The list of books for further reading has been expanded into a comprehensive bibliography of modern writings on Irish history. The chronology has been rewritten, updated, and much enlarged, so that it now amounts to a substantial supplement to the text. Finally, the index has been revised and extended both to include the new chapter and fill gaps in the original coverage.

The Great Irish Famine

edited by Cathal Póirtéir

This is the most wide-ranging series of essays ever published on the Great Irish Famine and will prove of lasting interest to the general reader. Leading historians, geographers – from Ireland, Britain and the United States – have assembled the most up-to-date research from a wide spectrum of disciplines, including medicine, folklore and literature, to give the fullest account yet of the background and consequences of the Famine. Contributors include Dr Kevin Whelan, Professor Mary Daly, Professor James Donnelly and Professor Cormac Ó Gráda.

The Great Irish Famine is the first major series of essays on the Famine to be published in Ireland for almost fifty years.

The Diary of an Irish Countryman, 1825–1835

A translation of Cín Lae Amhlaoibh by Tomás de Bhaildraithe

This diary is both a fascinating social history and a self-portrait of a most sensitive man.

It was written in Irish by Humphrey O'Sullivan, while living in Callan, Co. Kilkenny. He followed his father's calling when he became a hedgeschool master but later went on to become a prosperous businessman and philanthropist.

No aspect of life escaped his attention, from the dire poverty and degradation of the peasantry to the flora and fauna of the region.

Bobby Sands and the Tragedy of Northern Ireland

John M. Feehan

Bobby Sands captured the imagination of the world when, despite predictions, he was elected a Member of Parliament to the British House of Commons while still on hunger-strike in the Northern Ireland concentration camp of Long Kesh.

When he later died after sixty-six gruelling days of hunger he commanded more television, radio and newspaper coverage than papal visits or royal weddings.

In calm, restrained language John M. Feehan records the life of Bobby Sands with whom he had little sympathy at the beginning – though this was to change. At the same time he gives us an illuminating and crystal-clear account of the terrifying statelet of Northern Ireland today and of the fierce guerrilla warfare that is rapidly turning Northern Ireland into Britain's Vietnam.

My Village – My World

John M. Feehan

My Village – My World is a fascinating account of ordinary people in the countryside. It depicts a way of life that took thousands of years to evolve and mature and was destroyed in a single generation. As John M. Feehan says 'Nobody famous ever came from our village. None of its inhabitants ever achieved great public acclaim ... The people of our village could be described in government statistics as unskilled. That would be a false description. They were all highly skilled, whether in constructing privies or making coffins, digging drains, or cutting hedges, droving cattle or tending to stallions ...'

The SAS in Ireland

Raymond Murray

The SAS in Ireland traces the history of the British Army Special Air Services Regiment, the SAS, in Ireland over the past twenty years. It details their activities – intelligence gathering and surveillance, their links with British Intelligence, notably MI5 and MI6, their connection with sectarian murders and many other deaths.

Fr Raymond Murray is a respected commentator on events in the north of Ireland. In this book he analyses in detail the activities of the SAS and plain clothes soldiers in the Six Counties. His research leads him to the conclusion that in many instances the SAS engaged in a careful and organised shoot-to-kill policy.

Michael Collins – the Man who Won the War

T. Ryle Dwyer

In formally proposing the adoption of the Anglo-Irish Treaty on 19 December 1921 Arthur Griffith referred to Michael Collins as 'the man who won the War', much to the annoyance of the Defence Minister Cathal Brugha, who questioned whether Collins 'had ever fired a shot at any enemy of Ireland'.

Who was this Michael Collins, and what was his real role in the War of Independence? How was it that two sincere, selfless individuals like Griffith and Brugha, could differ so strongly about him?

This is the story of a charismatic rebel who undermined British morale and inspired Irish people with exploits both real and imaginary.